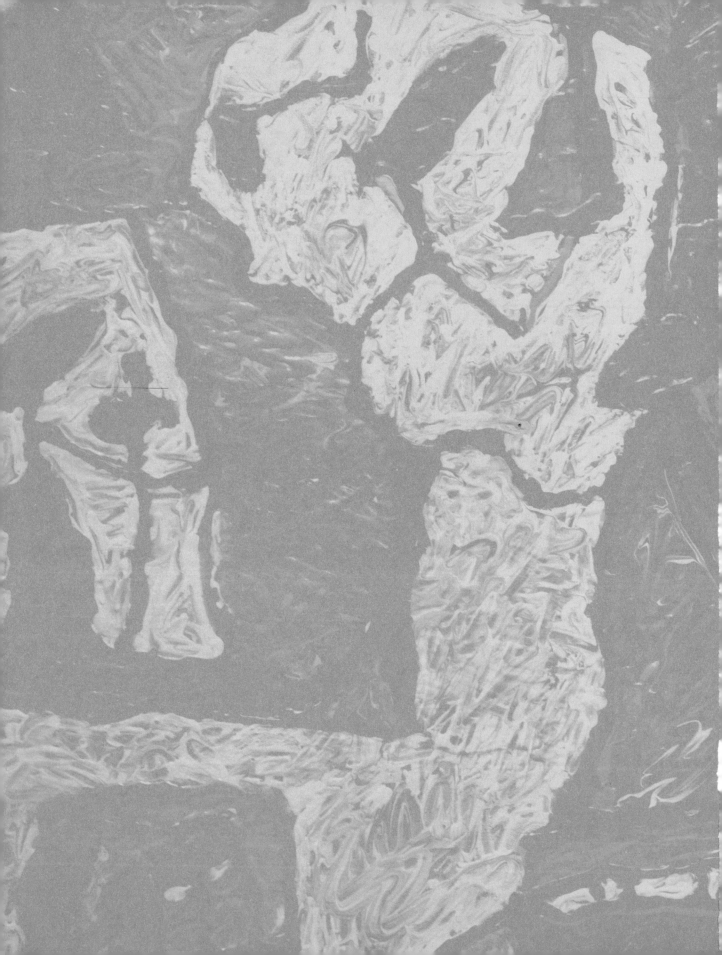

bis on main

ISBN: 978-0-615-39462-6

Library of Congress Cataloging-in-Publication Data is available on file.

Published by
Joe Vilardi / Bis on Main
10213 Main Street
Bellevue, WA 98004
www.bisonmain.com

In Association with:

James O. Fraioli
Culinary Book Creations LLC
PO Box 4066
Bellevue, Washington 98009

Designed by: *the*BookDesigners
(www.bookdesigners.com)

Printed in China through Globalink
(www.globalinkprinting.com)

10 9 8 7 6 5 4 3 2 1

bis on main

contemporary

northwest

cuisine

joe vilardi

with James O. Fraioli

Photography by Kathryn Barnard

dedication

To my mother, Dorothy,
who taught me the values of love and kindness,
and my first cooking lessons.
And to my two beautiful boys, Jack and Charlie.

acknowledgments

Chef Christopher Peterson for his contributions in creating
and compiling many of the recipes in this book.

The Bis on Main staff, for their years of dedication, support and service.

All the guests who have dined at Bis on Main,
especially our many great regulars.

James O. Fraioli, for his professional guidance
throughout the bookmaking process.

contents

joe's story

Many would say in the restaurant world's social pecking order, pot scrubbers peck at the bottom. If that's the case, it's where I started at age 14. Although I had to lie and say I was 16, my first employer, Raleigh House Caterers of Southfield, Michigan, was happy to have anyone who would come in and scrub endless piles of sheet pans, army pans and all sorts of pots and utensils. What they didn't expect was I would become the best pot washer they ever had. The cooks missed my talents when several months later the Hungarian Chef, Geza Lang, promoted me to "kitchen boy." Although I started at 70 cents an hour and pleaded for 10-cent raises along the way, one thing became clear: I was a worker and I would work hard for the rest of my life.

The Raleigh House was a great place to begin my life in the food-service business. For years, Sammy Lieberman ran the preeminent catering facility in the Detroit area, hosting dinners for more than 3,000 guests for the 'Big 3' and outside catering functions for up to 5,000. One time The Temptations performed in the big room and the waiters danced in the service hallway to "Ain't Too Proud to Beg." I remember the time the table we were serving from collapsed in the middle of the dining room—sending potatoes, vegetables, pots and the like crashing to the floor. This provided a lesson in what to do when the worst possible scenario plays out. There was also the time we had a large fundraising dinner for Bobby Kennedy. Secret Service agents busted my coworker and I after we slipped out to eat lunch, smoke cigarettes and listen to my eight-track tape player in my car.

The specialty of the house was Prime Rib Flambé, the presentation of which would be in a dimly lit dining room with the general manager, Frank, on the microphone introducing the chef at each carving station: "From Budapest, Hungary, Chef Geza Lang; from Marseilles, France, Chef Gene Ameriguan; from Salerno, Italy, Chef Giuseppe Calitano" (he was actually from Queens). Then, in unison, the chefs would each ignite a pot filled with a warmed fifth of Cointreau and pour the liqueure over a mountain of prime rib roasts, sending the irredescent flames skyward. The lights would come on and we kitchen boys, in our crisp white jackets and aprons, became part of the production line, as legions of tuxedoed waiters and waitresses came through the line, plates in hand, receiving first the slab of beef, then the au jus,

after which we added the peas and potatoes and off to the guests they went.

The Raleigh House sustained me off and on through junior high, high school and beyond. After high school, I moved to Ypsilanti, Michigan, and enrolled at Eastern Michigan University, despite my father questioning me: "Why the hell do you need to go to college?" During my year at Eastern, I landed my first server job at Perkins Cake & Steak, waiting tables from midnight until 8 a.m. a few days a week. This job turned out to be a very formative period in my life and had little to do with the classes I was taking at school. The menagerie of drunks, hippies, freaks and loners I met on my graveyard shifts provided some of those real life lessons you hear about and welded friendships with a unique group of Ann Arborites with whom I am still friends almost 40 years later.

Keep in mind, this was the early '70s and it was not unusual for a young man like myself to have hair long past my shoulders, which I did. Such hairstyles, while very cool, didn't jibe with restaurant work at the time. So for Perkins, and a subsequent stint at one of Ann Arbor's best fine-dining restaurants, I would pin my hair to the top of my head and don a short-hair wig for work. This made for some good comedy when coworkers first saw me without my wig.

The summer after my freshman year, I moved back home and returned to work at the Raleigh House, this time in the stockroom assisting Lloyd, a wonderful, large man who kept a bottle of whiskey in his desk drawer. My job was to deliver to the different kitchen stations long lists of fruits, vegetables, meats, fish, dry goods and so on, and to also receive, stock and rotate the product that was delivered every day. That summer was an especially busy one for Sammy and Co., and I recall working 36 days in a row at one stretch without the bothersome element of overtime pay and all that.

It was during that long stretch I returned home to my parents' house after another 12-hour day, tired, cranky and ready to do nothing, when my older brother Bob (who had no car at the time) asked me to drive him to our oldest brother's apartment about five miles away. I have always been an easy touch, so though I protested and described my fatigue, I eventually caved in and drove Bobby to Frank's apartment.

When we arrived behind Frank's apartment, an attractive young girl appeared on a bicycle. Bob insisted I pull alongside so he could chat with her. Well, wouldn't you know, it was me who ended up going to dinner with this sweet thing, who happened to be visiting from New Orleans to see her aunt.

Six months later, I gathered my 19-year-old belongings and moved to the Crescent City and into a Garden District apartment with the afore-mentioned bicyclist. Prior to meeting her, I had it in my mind I was going to move somewhere, probably California, but because of that car ride I gave my brother, I found myself in New Orleans. This event set in motion a series of events that changed my life forever and, 25 years later, resulted in the opening of Bis on Main.

I will never forget the night I drove into New Orleans on Interstate 55—all that water, and the city lights. I wasn't in Kansas anymore. Without cell phone or GPS, I found Monica and our little apartment on Prytania.

The next morning, I got up, donned my infamous wig and headed to the French Quarter, where in a matter of hours, landed a busboy job at Arnaud's on Bienville Street. At the time, Arnaud's had over 300 a la carte items on their menu. Some had not been ordered in years. Some of the chefs had no idea how to make them. After a short time, and (finally) a haircut, I moved on and ended up with a waiter job at the Rib Room of the Royal Orleans Hotel.

It was there that I met my lifelong friend and cofounder of Bis, Michel Fredj.

Michel was a dining room captain at the Rib Room. He was only 25, but had already traveled the world and was on his second wife, a fiery redhead from Paris named Brigitte. We quickly became friends and Michel schooled me on the finer points of the restaurant business. Shortly thereafter, Michel and Brigitte opened their own restaurant in the French Quarter off Jackson Square. I lent a hand helping them open, and after 18 months in New Orleans, went back home to live with my parents in suburban Detroit.

Of course, Michel and I kept in touch. After running their restau-rant for a few years, he and his wife returned to France and pur-chased a chalet and restaurant on Mont Salève, overlooking Geneva,

Switzerland, and Lac Léman. After they were established, they invited me to come for an extended visit. I ended spending nearly six months at the Chalet de la Croix, above the small village of Monnetier-Salève We would get up early in the crisp mountain air and head to the local markets to buy meat, fish and produce for the Chalet restaurant, while sampling the most incredible food along the way—cheese, meat, fruit, vegetables, herbs and wine.

I also drank a lot of coffee, played chess, read a ton of books and got acquainted with the group of hang gliders Michel jumped off the side of Mont Salève with. I even tried it myself a couple times on a bunny hill. I met some of the lovely girls from the village. I went to Paris. I went to Italy (twice). 'La vie a la montagne,' as we liked to call it, was a great experience—but after six months, I went back to good old Detroit.

By this time, my parents, Frank (a home builder) and Dorothy (housewife and great mom), my sisters, Pam and Suzanne and brother Bob had all moved west, to California. That left oldest brother Frank and I the only Vilardi's in Detroit.

Frank died unexpectedly in 1979, and it was then that the rest of my family convinced me to join them in Los Angeles.

I moved to an apartment in Burbank with the intention of 'learning the business' from my dad who was in the midst of building hundreds of condo's in the San Fernando Valley. It soon became apparent that the building business and I were not meant to be. On an evening when the whole family went to one of my father's favorite Italian restaurants, La Maganette, on Sunset Strip, I learned that the Maitre' d, Louie, was retiring and I beseeched my father to talk to the owners and ask them to give me a shot at his job.

To everyone's surprise, the owners, cousins from NYC, Johnny (Beans) Pezzulo and Johnny (Popcorn) Pellegrino, did give me a shot. It turned out I was pretty damned good at running their dining room. Before I knew it, I was taking care of Sammy Davis Jr., Frank Sinatra Jr., Bette Midler, Ricardo Montalban and many others.

After a couple years—and a short stint in between trying to help an oil heiress open a restaurant in Scottsdale—I had an opportunity for a waiter's job at the legendary Palm Restaurant on Santa Monica Boulevard. During the '70s through the '90s, the Palm was the *best* job in Los Angeles. They would go years without hiring a single front-of-the-house person, so when one of their waiters, Cosmo, informed me of an impending opening, I went and talked to the late Gigi del Maestro and he gave me the job! I had never made so much money in my life. And then there was the whole Hollywood scene. Imagine someone famous from Hollywood in the '70s and '80s and I probably waited on them. Not only that, the Palm went against every restaurant principle I had ever learned. The waiters drank on the job at will. We smoked in the dining room by the kitchen door and put our cigarettes out on the sawdust-covered floor while whistling at the gorgeous girls on their way to the ladies room. There was no menu for the guests. We recited the dishes to each table and, believe me, we never mentioned the inexpensive items available. We rushed customers in and out like you cannot believe, despite being the most expensive restaurant in the city. And then there was the scene: movie stars, rock stars, athletes, producers, directors and studio heads. Anyone who was anyone in LA during that time came through the Palm.

I spent more than five years at the Palm, after which I was fortunate to be employed at some of Los Angeles' finest restaurants of the time, including the original Spago above Sunset Strip, Michel Richard's Citrus, and Mark Peel and Nancy Silverton's Campanile/La Brea Bakery. While at the original Spago, Wolfgang allowed me to act as an unpaid apprentice a couple days a week in the kitchen. I worked with some wonderful and talented chefs who taught me some of the basic skills and techniques I use to this day. I also learned a few recipes that have become staples of the Bis menu.

When I worked for Michel Richard, who made some of the finest food I have ever tasted in my life, he would always ask me, "You worked at Spago, but they do not make food like we do here." I would immediately reply, "No Chef. Certainly not!" And it was true. They were not the same, but they were both great.

Around the same time, I met an lovely English actress who was vacationing in LA. Within a year we were married. I also found myself keeping very busy while satisfying eclectic tastes. I became involved in public radio, first volunteering and then working for radio station KCRW-FM in Santa Monica. I hosted a late-night music show for four years and was also the music librarian during the day. I also opened my own fledgling (yet successful) catering business, which I ran out of my Beverly Hills apartment where I lived for more than 10 years, and worked part time at Campanile Restaurant. I also became the occasional private chef for a wealthy Italian family who spent a few months a year at their Bel Air estate. My job was to come in and prepare lunches and dinners when they had guests in town, and to accompany them on their annual ski trips and summer vacations where I would do all the cooking, make all the arrangements, drive the car and so on.

In 1993, after the Rodney King riots in LA, the company my wife worked for offered her a big promotion and bonus if we would move to Utah. The opportunity for a new adventure and the allure of being able to afford our own house, combined with the questionable future of life in LA, had its effect. We took the bait and left the hectic LA lifestyle for Orem, Utah, 35 miles south of Salt Lake City.

I grew to love Utah, absolutely one of the most beautiful places on earth. To this day I treasure the year and a half I spent there. There was little, however, for me to do in the 'Mormon Bible Belt.' I kept myself busy meeting the neighbors, who gave me endless advice on getting my lawn really lush and green, and making extravagant dinners for my weary wife after a long day at work. I landed a weekly music show on

one of Salt Lake City's public radio stations, and I traveled to LA for a few weeks at a time to cook for the Italians and to arrange their lavish vacations to Lake Tahoe and Lake Powell.

Eventually my wife's company closed their Orem office and encouraged us to move to their home base in Montreal, an option I mulled over for a full nanosecond before deciding: not a chance in hell.

We considered staying in Utah, but there wasn't a future there for us, and the thought of going back to LA did not sit well. We visited friends who had relocated to Seattle, and then in November 1993 we sold our home and moved to the great Pacific Northwest. A few months later I landed the maitre d'/manager position at one of Seattle's oldest and finest Italian restaurants, Il Terrazzo Carmine, where I spent the next four years catering to the Who's Who of Seattle.

By then, my old friend Michel, had moved back to New Orleans and established a chain of very successful restaurants named Louisiana Pizza Kitchen. He was a key player in the Louisiana restaurant scene and would still be today, had it not been for a very sad series of events that convinced him to leave New Orleans. When he decided he'd had enough, Michel sold off his half of the business to his partner and came to Seattle with the intention of us opening a restaurant together.

On June 1, 1998, Michel and I took ownership of a little sandwich shop on Bellevue's Old Main Street. After a modest remodel, Bis on Main opened its doors on September 21, 1998. We took the name (we were desperate to come up with something apropos) from the French and Italian, 'bis', meaning two, twice or another. Michel is French and

I am Italian American. The two us were a 'bis' of sorts. Michel came up with the 'on Main' bit. I often think back on the fact that if I had not given my brother that ride so many years ago, I would have never moved to New Orleans and as a result would have never met Michel and there would never have been a Bis on Main.

We had been open for about one year when Michel decided he missed life in the south, and moved back to Atlanta.

With the help of a prominent patron, I bought Michel out of his share of the restaurant and became the sole owner, which instantly translated into 80 hours a week and plenty of stress. The joys of the restaurant business.

At the same time, my wife decided she'd seen enough of my routine and asked for a divorce. And a few weeks later my father took ill, passing away just before Christmas.

But now, after 12 years, I can honestly say I've been fortunate. My hard work has translated into good luck. Bis on Main continues to be a beacon of fine dining in Bellevue and the greater Seattle area. My countless days and nights at the front desk of my restaurant have afforded me the opportunity to meet and get to know some of the finest people in our community. It has also allowed me the opportunity to demonstrate the skills I've gathered from my days scrubbing pots at the Raleigh House, through my time in France, Los Angeles and Seattle.

I continue to try every day to make Bis on Main the very best it can be and to instill in our fine staff the ideals of quality and service, and the honest, measured approach to restaurants that I have learned in my many years.

My success and this book, among other things, would never have been imaginable without the encouragement, devotion and divine patronage of our many, many regular guests who have complemented my life and that of our staff these many years. For this, we are all forever grateful. Thank you and God bless.

—Joe Vilardi, Owner, Bis on Main

Cocktails & Hors D'Oeuvres

Vesper

Ingredients

2 ounces vodka

1 ounce gin

¾ ounce lillet (white)

Orange twist

Method

Fill a martini shaker with ice. Measure the vodka, gin and lillet, and add to the shaker. Using a bar spoon, slowly stir the drink for about 25 seconds. Strain into a chilled martini glass. Garnish with an orange twist.

Note: The Vesper was invented and named by James Bond, 007, in the 1953 novel *Casino Royale*.

Bis Rye Manhattan 1 SERVING

2 ounces Russell's Reserve 6-year rye whiskey

1 ounce Antica vermouth

4 dashes orange bitters

1 slice of orange peel

Fill a pint glass with ice. Measure the whiskey, vermouth and bitters into the ice. Stir gently in circular motion for 25 seconds. Pour contents through a martini strainer into a chilled martini glass. Hold the piece of orange peel over the drink in one hand and a cigarette lighter in the other. Carefully heat the peel so the oils release. The peel should flame up. As soon as it does, drop the peel into the drink and serve.

Negroni 1 SERVING

1 ounce Miller's gin

1 ounce Martini & Rossi sweet vermouth

1 ounce Campari

Splash of Angostura bitters

Orange twist

Measure the gin, sweet vermouth, and Campari and pour into a rocks glass filled with ice. Add the bitters and garnish with an orange twist.

Note: You can enhance your Negroni by slicing a wide piece of orange peel and warming the outer skin with a lighter and then squeezing the peel over your drink while holding a lighter in the other hand. The oils from the peel will flare and add a unique flavor to the drink.

Joe's Mojito 1 SERVING

6 fresh mint sprigs, leaves only

3 lime wedges

½ ounce Cointreau

2½ ounces Ten Cane rum

½ ounce lime sour mix (see page 7)

Fill a pint glass with ice, mint leaves and 2 lime wedges. Add Cointreau. Use a muddle stick and vigorously mash the ingredients. Add more ice and pour in the rum. Top off with lime sour and garnish with a lime wedge.

The LeLand 1 SERVING

2 ounces vodka

½ ounce simple syrup

7 fresh basil leaves (reserve one large
leaf for garnish)

3 slices of cucumber

Juice of ½ lemon

Fill a martini shaker with ice. Measure the vodka and simple syrup and add to the shaker. Tear 6 basil leaves and add to the shaker along with the cucumber slices. Using a muddle stick, vigorously muddle the ingredients for 15 seconds to release the flavors. Strain the contents through a fine, small-mesh strainer and into a chilled martini glass. Take the remaining basil leaf and slap it between the palms of your hand. This will also release a burst of basil aromatics. Lay the leaf so half of it touches the inside edge of the glass and the other half floats on the drink.

Note: Simple syrup is equal parts sugar and water heated until the sugar dissolves and then cooled.

Silk Teddy 1 SERVING

2 ounces vodka

1½ ounces St. Germain liquor

½ ounce lemon sour mix (see below)

Squeeze of fresh lemon

Sugar, to coat rim

Lemon twist

Fill a martini shaker with ice. Measure the vodka, St. Germain, lemon sour and fresh lemon juice. Shake 32 times. Dip the rim of a chilled martini glass into a dish of sugar so the entire rim is covered. Strain into a chilled martini glass. Garnish with a lemon twist.

Sour Mix MAKES 3 CUPS

2 cups water

1 cup granulated sugar

1 cup lemon (or lime) juice

In a heavy-bottomed sauce pot, add the water sugar and lemon (or lime) juice over medium heat. Bring to a boil. Remove from heat and refrigerate contents. The mix will store for up to 2 weeks.

Brigitte

Ingredients

1½ ounces Miller's gin

4 dashes peach bitters

1 ounce ruby red grapefruit juice

½ ounce St. Germain

1 ounce rose champagne

Orange twist

Method

Fill a martini shaker with ice. Measure in the gin, bitters, grapefruit juice and St. Germain. Shake for 15 seconds. Strain into a cold martini glass. Top with the rose champagne, and float the orange twist.

Ingredients

½ ounce triple sec

Wedge of lemon

2 ounces pear brandy

1 ounce lemon sour mix (see page 7)

Lemon twist

Method

In a martini shaker with ice, measure in the triple sec and add the lemon wedge. Muddle vigorously. Add pear brandy and lemon sour mix, and mix well. Strain into a martini glass and garnish with lemon twist.

Twice-Baked
Fingerling Potatoes

4-6 SERVINGS

Ingredients

1 pound rock salt

2 pounds fingerling potatoes, rinsed

½ pound bacon, thinly cut

2 tablespoons unsalted butter, cut into small cubes

1 tablespoon crème fraiche (see page 151)

2 tablespoons heavy cream

1 tablespoon kosher salt

1 teaspoon black pepper

2 tablespoons fresh chives, chopped

Method

PREHEAT THE OVEN TO 425°F.

Place the rock salt in a baking dish or roasting pan, large enough to hold the potatoes. Place the potatoes on top and cover with a lid or sheet of foil. Place in the oven and roast until done, approximately 45 minutes. Allow the potatoes to cool completely before handling.

While the potatoes are roasting, lay strips of bacon on a sheet pan and place into the oven. Cook until crispy. Drain and reserve 1 tablespoon of the bacon fat. Chop or break the bacon into small pieces.

Once potatoes are cooled, cut them in half lengthwise. Using a teaspoon, carefully scoop out the insides of the potatoes, making sure to leave a little along the edges and bottom so the potato holds its shape. In a mixing bowl, combine the potato insides, bacon, bacon fat, butter, crème fraiche, heavy cream, salt and pepper. Mix together with a fork or potato masher. Add the chives and mix again briefly. If you do not have a piping bag, simply place the mixture in a ziplock bag and snip off one of the bottom corners with a scissor.

Pipe the desired amount of mixture back into each potato half. Place the stuffed potatoes on a baking sheet and place in the oven for about 7 minutes.

To Serve: Transfer the rock salt to a small serving platter and arrange the potatoes on top.

Note: Everybody loves twice-baked potatoes, and we have our favorite toppings at the restaurant, such as cheese and caviar. Don't be afraid to try different toppings. The potatoes can also be made one day in advance.

Ingredients

1 box of frozen phylo dough

2 pounds mixed fresh mushrooms, preferably wild

½ pound unsalted butter, divided

2 tablespoons olive oil

1 tablespoon garlic, minced

2 tablespoons white wine

1 tablespoon fresh thyme leaves, chopped

Salt and black pepper, to taste

½ cup grated Gruyere cheese (course, not fine)

Method

PREHEAT THE OVEN TO 425°F.

Completely thaw the phylo dough at room temperature in the box. Remove the stems from the mushrooms and slice thinly, making sure the different types are cut to similar sizes. Melt 3 tablespoons of the butter and olive oil in a large sauté pan over high heat. When the butter has foamed, add the mushrooms and toss several times. Allow the mushrooms to cook down, tossing intermittently. Cook the mushrooms until all the liquid has evaporated and the mushrooms start to lightly brown. Add the garlic, white wine, chopped thyme, salt and pepper. Cook a couple more minutes. Remove from heat and cool completely. When cool, roughly chop the mushrooms and combine them with the Gruyere cheese.

Next, melt the remaining butter in a small dish so it can be brushed over the phylo dough. Remove the phylo dough from the box, place on a cutting board, and carefully unfold the dough. Lay a loose piece of plastic wrap over the phylo, followed by a lightly damp cloth. This will keep the phylo from cracking while you work with it. Working quickly, remove one sheet of the phylo and re-cover the rest. Gently brush some of the melted butter over the surface of the dough. Add one more sheet on top of the first and lightly butter as well. With a sharp knife, cut the sheet into 6 strips. On the bottom of each strip, place 1½ tablespoons of the mushroom-cheese mixture. Starting with the end closest to you, begin folding upwards, creating a triangle shape. Brush a little more butter on top of each finished triangle and place on a baking sheet. Bake for 5 to 7 minutes, or until the phylo starts to brown slightly.

To Serve: Remove the triangles from baking sheet and arrange on a platter.

Note: The triangles can be made one day in advance. Make sure to cover with plastic and refrigerate. Bake before serving.

Ingredients

3 heads of red Belgian endive

½ pound sushi-grade ahi tuna, skin & blood line removed, diced in ½-inch cubes

4 tablespoons soy sauce

1 teaspoon fresh-grated ginger pulp (done with micro-plane or small side of a cheese grater)

3 tablespoons sesame oil

2 tablespoons rice vinegar

2 tablespoons mirin

2 tablespoons Sriracha (a hot sauce found in most grocery stores)

1½ scallions, finely chopped

25 cilantro leaves (or shiso leaves) for garnish

Method

On a cutting board, slice the bottom of the Belgian endive heads so each individual leaf can be removed. After each successive layer of leaves are peeled away, slice a little more off the root end to keep removing the leaves. When all the leaves are removed, plunge them into a bowl of slightly salted ice water. This will crisp the leaves and keep them from discoloring.

Next, in a plastic or stainless-steel mixing bowl, combine the tuna, soy sauce, ginger, sesame oil, rice vinegar, mirin, Sriracha and scallions. Fold together gently with a rubber spatula or wooden spoon so as not to crush or break apart the tuna. This should be done no more than one hour in advance. Cover with plastic and keep chilled until serving.

To Serve: Remove the endive leaves from the ice water, drain and pat dry on paper towels. Place a generous tablespoon of the tuna mixture in the root end of each endive leaf. Garnish the tuna with one cilantro leaf on top. Arrange on a serving platter.

Note: We sometimes like to wrap butter lettuce leaves around the tuna and endive, and add a bit of wasabi paste.

Stuffed Zucchini Blossoms with Fromage Blanc

Ingredients

2 quarts oil, for frying

2 tablespoons heavy cream

½ cup fromage blanc cheese (or goat cheese)

Zest of 1 lemon

1 teaspoon fresh chives, finely minced

1 teaspoon black pepper

12 zucchini squash blossoms

2 teaspoons kosher salt

½ cup all-purpose flour

2 cups panko bread crumbs, pulse in a food processor 6 times

5 whole eggs, beaten

Method

In a heavy-bottomed pot, add the oil over medium-high heat, until it reaches 350°F (use a candy thermometer). In a food processor, add the heavy cream, fromage blanc, lemon zest, chives and black pepper. Run machine until the cheese whips and aerates, about 1 minute. Transfer the mixture to a piping bag with a medium-sized tip (or use a Ziplock bag with a corner snipped with a scissor). Reserve the mixture in the refrigerator.

Carefully remove the pistils from the inside of the zucchini blossoms. This is done by gently spreading the petals apart at the top and plucking them out with a pair of tweezers. (Note: do not do this too far in advance or the blossoms will quickly begin to wilt.)

Once the pistils are removed, pipe the cheese mixture inside by gently holding the petals open, easing the tip of the pastry bag about one-third of the way into the blossom, and squeeze about 1½ tablespoons of the mixture inside. The blossom should be slightly plumped towards

the bottom, but not filled to the top. Gently twist the top of the petals to close them a bit.

Breading the blossoms: In one large pan, add half the salt to the flour. In another large pan, add the remaining salt to the panko. Roll the blossoms in the flour first, dusting off the excess. (Note: Try not to let the flour get inside the blossoms.) Next, dip them in the egg. (Note: It's best to pour the egg in something narrow like a tall water glass, making it easier to dip the blossoms.) Next, gently roll them in the panko, coating them well.

Frying the blossoms: Carefully add them to a deep-fryer or deep-frying pot filled with hot oil. (Caution: Working with very hot oil can be dangerous, so use extreme caution.) Fry the blossoms until just golden brown, about 2 minutes. (Note: If the blossoms are fried too long, they can burst.) Remove the blossoms and drain on paper towels.

To Serve: Arrange the blossoms on a serving platter or in a basket and serve warm.

Note: When the farmers market in Bellevue is in full swing, we love getting zucchini blossoms. We serve them simply in a basket with some lemon wedges or a little aioli, but you can stuff them with crab, shrimp or any kind of cheese you like. They are delicious chopped up raw in risotto too.

The success of Bis on Main is tied to the basics of customer satisfaction, customer recognition, consistently great food, excellent service and, most importantly, a friendly, knowledgeable and tenured staff who deliver an exceptional product to the table every day.

Kusshi Oysters on the Half Shell with Vesper Mignonette

Ingredients

1 tablespoon finely minced shallots

¼ teaspoon cracked black pepper

2 tablespoons vodka

1 tablespoon gin

4 tablespoons rice wine vinegar

1 tablespoon lillet blanc

2 dozen kusshi oysters

Crushed ice

1 lemon, cut into 8 wedges, pith and seeds removed, ends squared

Method

In a small bowl, mix the shallots, pepper, vodka, gin, rice vinegar and lillet. Combine thoroughly and chill.

With an oyster knife, shuck the oysters. When popped open, carefully run the shucker along the top inside surface of the shell to remove any connective tissue. Slide the shucker underneath the oyster to remove the mussel that connects the body to the shell. (Note: The trick is to stay close to the shell while trying to avoid piercing the oyster.) Remove any broken pieces of shell, particularly along the edges.

To Serve: These oysters are meant to be served extremely cold. Arrange a layer of crushed ice on a chilled serving platter. Place the cold mignonette in a small bowl in the center of the ice. Arrange the oysters in a desirable pattern, carefully nestling them into the ice. Place the lemon wedges on the platter in the same manner and serve.

the **bis** philosophy

When I arrived in Seattle in November 1993, I knew little about the fine-dining scene. After one month, I began looking for work. During my quest, it became clear which restaurants ranked at the top and which did not. It was also clear that just about every one of those highly ranked restaurants were located in Seattle and not in Bellevue, Kirkland or other Eastside suburban communities. When I obtained gainful employment at one of those premier restaurants, another observation became apparent—many of the customers who headed into town for dinner were from Bellevue and the Eastside. At the time, dining in Bellevue or anywhere on the Eastside was considered as glamorous as a root canal.

Before opening Bis on Main, one well-known physician told me, "You might do a little lunch trade, but don't count on people coming for dinner." The first night he visited Bis on Main, he had to wait 30 minutes for a table.

Another said to me, "You're opening on the Eastside? What's your '*hook*' going to be? You'll need something to get people in." That perplexed me. I thought good food, a well-rounded wine list, fair pricing and friendly, attentive service should be enough.

Fortunately, I resisted the urge to have servers on roller skates singing opera. I just stuck to the basics. This turned out to be a good choice for me.

The success of Bis is tied to just that, the basics: Customer satisfaction, customer recognition, consistently great food, excellent service and, most importantly, a friendly, knowledgeable and tenured staff who deliver an exceptional product to the table every day.

Customers always comment on what a great staff we have, and it is true. Our employees stick with Bis far longer than the industry standard and I know it is tied to more than just my handsome charm. The key is finding a team who buys into our ideals and understand that shortcuts and cutting corners is a one-way ticket to restaurant oblivion. It is also my job is to make certain the staff has a great work environment. They need to make a good living, they need to know they are appreciated, and they have to feel confident about what we serve and how we go about serving it.

I like to think that Bis delivers not only consistently great food, wine and service to our guests, but also value. We like to hit 'singles,' not a 'home run' every time. It is more important to us that our customers leave happy and feeling that they got what they paid for, or more. We want people to come back—often. Our motto is, "Underpromise and overdeliver."

We also like to operate with a sense of humor rather than a stuffy air of self-importance. A typical scenario is a nice couple who arrive without reservations on a busy night, sheepishly asking if there might be a table available. Well, I say, we are very busy but do have a seat for the beautiful lady, but can't help the gentleman.

Maintaining the consistency and style of Bis on Main is also my job. We all know it is impossible to be perfect, but it is important that we start each day with that intention. If a customer has a negative comment on a dish, chances are that is what I will have for my dinner that night. Customers have many choices when deciding where to dine. The success of our restaurant is the customer who has been coming for years and has never had a bad meal or thinks we have the best staff in the city. Coming to Bis on Main should never be a crap shoot. It should be a slam dunk.

Our ambience is another responsibility of mine. Since the restaurant's inception, in lieu of fresh flowers on the tables, I have adorned the walls with modern Northwest art, all of which I personally select. Over the years, I have purchased the lion's share of what is on display, but we still rent a number of paintings from our friends at the Seattle Art Museum. It's a wonderful way to support our local artists and the museum, and guests appreciate the new paintings we showcase at the restaurant.

I also personally select the music guests hear while dining with us. All of our playlists are culled from my personal collection of albums and CDs, which I have assembled over the years, dating back to my days as a DJ on public radio in Santa Monica.

There are many other duties I perform, far too many to list. Nevertheless, it's these many responsibilities that makes Bis what it is today—a successful and thriving restaurant on Seattle's Eastside. I feel I've created an inviting place where guests, whether casual or business, can enjoy exceptional food with impeccable service while feeling comfortable. More importantly, I want Bis on Main to be an extension of my home. I want it to be my "Cheers."

I invite you to experience Bis on Main. For those who already have, I welcome you back.   —J.V.

Baked Eggs with Potatoes, Bacon & Caramelized Onions

6 SERVINGS

Ingredients

1 pound thick-cut bacon, sliced into ¼-inch-wide strips

2 yellow onions, peeled and julienned (thinly sliced) ⅛ inch thick

2½ tablespoons kosher salt

2 teaspoons black pepper

2 tablespoons minced garlic

2½-pound fingerling potatoes, washed and cut into ⅛-inch-thick rounds

2 tablespoons unsalted butter

½ cup white wine

½ cup chicken stock

1 tablespoon red pepper flake

3 cups heavy cream

2 tablespoons chopped fresh thyme

12 large eggs, room temperature

Method

PREHEAT THE OVEN TO 450°F.

In a large sauté pan, over medium-high heat, cook the bacon strips until they are almost crispy, about 8 minutes. Remove the bacon with a slotted spoon and transfer them to a large ovenproof baking dish and set aside. To the sauté pan, add the onions, ½ tablespoon salt, ½ teaspoon black pepper and garlic, stirring frequently. Cook until the onions are well-caramelized, about 10 minutes. Remove the onions and transfer to the baking dish. Add the potato rounds and butter. Cook the potatoes until they have started to brown and slightly soften, about 8 minutes. Add the white wine to the sauté pan and reduce for 20 seconds. Add the chicken stock, chili flakes, cream and chopped thyme. Bring to a simmer and thicken the cream slightly. Pour into the baking dish.

Add the remaining salt and pepper to the baking dish, stir all the contents, and gently crack the eggs, one at a time, over the top of the mixture. Make sure the yolks don't break and each egg has its own place to settle in. Place the baking dish in the oven uncovered and bake until the whites are just set and the yolks are still fairly runny, about 10 minutes. Remove from the oven.

To Serve: This dish is meant to be served family style, where everyone scoops out what they want. If you'd like to serve the dish, use a large serving spoon and carefully scoop underneath the area of two eggs, making sure to get the contents that lay beneath the eggs. Try not to break the yolks, and place in individual serving bowls.

Foie Gras with Pineapple Gastrique, Honey-Roasted Macadamia & Broiche

6 SERVINGS

Ingredients

Pineapple Gastrique

4 tablespoons granulated sugar

1 cup fresh pineapple juice

2 tablespoons fresh lemon juice

1 tablespoon white wine vinegar

½ teaspoon kosher salt

Pineapple Relish

1 cup fresh pineapple, very small dice

¼ cup fresh jicama, peeled, very small dice

1½ tablespoons fresh cilantro, chopped

½ teaspoon fresh ginger, peeled and finely minced

1 tablespoon red bell pepper, very small dice

1 teaspoon fresh lemon juice

½ teaspoon kosher salt

¼ teaspoon black pepper

Foie Gras & Foie Gras Butter

1 (1½ pound "A" Grade) foie gras lobe (order online or special order from gourmet shop)

1 tablespoon kosher salt

1 teaspoon black pepper

¼ pound unsalted butter, room temperature

1 loaf of brioche bread, cut into 18 small 2-inch-long by ¼-inch-thick triangles

⅓ cup honey-and-salt-roasted macadamia nuts (available at high-quality markets)

Method

Pineapple Gastrique: In a small saucepan, over medium-high heat, add the sugar. Stirring frequently, melt the sugar until a light brown color is achieved. Quickly add the pineapple juice, lemon juice, wine vinegar and salt. Whisk until incorporated. (Note: The sugar will first caramelize to the pan, getting very hard. This is okay.) Keep whisking. Within a couple minutes, the sugar will re-melt, and the liquid will thicken. Cook until thick bubbles form on the surface, about 4 minutes. Cool the liquid and reserve.

Pineapple Relish: In a mixing bowl, combine the pineapple, jicama, cilantro, ginger, bell pepper, lemon juice, salt and pepper. Mix thoroughly and chill.

Foie gras: Observe where the small and large lobe meet. Firmly grip the foie and carefully split the lobes apart. Gently remove the sinew and blood veins without damaging the lobes. (Note: A pair of tweezers or small kitchen pliers works well.) Once deveined, lay the lobes on a cutting board and cut six 3 to 3½ ounces crosswise steaks (reserve the scraps). Be sure the ends are flat, so the steaks sear properly. Re-chill the foie gras steaks.

Foie gras butter: Place a sauté pan over high heat. Season the reserved foie gras scraps with salt and pepper. When the pan is hot, add the pieces directly to the pan. This will generate a lot of smoke as the fat renders. Saute the pieces for 45 seconds, turning them once. Keep the fat in the pan. Remove the scrap pieces and let cool for 5 minutes. Add the scraps to a food processor with the butter, and run the machine for 1 minute. Chill and reserve the butter. Return the pan to medium-high heat. Place the brioche triangles in the pan and brown on both sides, about 2 minutes. Reserve at room temperature.

Season the foie gras steaks with salt and pepper. Place a large sauté pan up over medium-high heat. Once the pan is hot, add the steaks and sear until brown, about 1 minute. Turn the steaks and continue to cook another 45 seconds. Transfer the steaks to paper towels, and discard all but ½ teaspoon of fat from the pan. Add the macadamia nuts and pineapple gastrique. When the gastrique bubbles, remove from heat and add 1 tablespoon of the reserved foie gras butter. Season with salt and pepper.

To Serve: On each of 6 appetizer plates, arrange 3 brioche croutons, stacked neatly at 2 o'clock on the plate. Place 2 tablespoons of pineapple relish at 10 o'clock, and the foie gras at 6 o'clock. Spoon some of the sauce on and around the foie gras and serve.

Note: Make sure the foie gras is very cold when working with it, otherwise the fat will melt from the heat of your hands.

Ingredients

Sausage

1½ tablespoons minced garlic

1 teaspoon kosher salt

¼ teaspoon black pepper

1½ teaspoon fresh-chopped basil

1½ teaspoon fresh-chopped oregano

1½ teaspoon fresh-chopped thyme

1½ teaspoon fresh-chopped Italian parsley

1 teaspoon fennel frond, chopped

½ tablespoon red pepper flakes

1 pound pork butt, ½-inch dice

1½ tablespoons Sriracha (hot sauce)

6½ tablespoons red wine

Clams

4 tablespoons olive oil

2 tablespoons minced garlic

2 teaspoons red chili flakes

6 Roma tomatoes, seeded, ½-inch dice

1 cup dry white wine

3 pounds Manila clams, rinsed under cold water for 15 minutes

2 tablespoons fresh-chopped marjoram

2 tablespoons unsalted butter

Method

PREHEAT THE OVEN TO 425°F.

Sausage: In a mixing bowl, combine the garlic, salt, pepper, basil, oregano, thyme, parsley, fennel frond and red pepper flakes. Mix thoroughly and rub the pork with the spice-herb mixture. Make sure to evenly coat the pork. Add the hot sauce and red wine. Toss well. Transfer the sausage mixture into a food processor, add one ice cube and pulse for 1 minute. (Note: Do not ove-process or the fats will melt and the sausage will lose its texture.) Remove from the processor and form mixture into 1-inch balls. Place the sausage on a parchment-lined baking sheet and roast in the oven for 8 minutes. Remove and set aside.

In two large sauté pans or a clam pot, over high heat, add the olive oil. When hot, divide the chopped garlic evenly between the pans, and sauté briefly, about 1 minute. Add the chili flakes and the clams, tossing several times. Add the tomatoes, sausage and white wine. Bring to a simmer and cover until clams open, about 3 minutes. Uncover and add the marjoram and butter. Swirl and toss until the butter is melted.

To Serve: Remove any unopened clams and serve family style in a large pot with plenty of bread for dipping.

Red Curry Mussels with Bell Peppers, Ginger, Mint & Coconut Gremolata

6 SERVINGS

Ingredients

Gremolata

2 tablespoons chopped candied ginger (found in bulk-food section of grocery store)

⅛ cup fresh mint leaves

2 tablespoons ground sweet coconut

Mussels

1 large red potato, washed, skin on, small diced

2 tablespoons olive oil

1 large red bell pepper, seeded and cut into ½-inch squares

3 peeled shallots, cut into thinly sliced rounds

4 tablespoons red curry paste (found in Asian foods section of grocery store)

3 pounds live mussels, cleaned and de-bearded

⅛ cup white wine

4 ounces clam juice

1 cup heavy cream

2 cans coconut milk

⅛ cup fresh basil leaves, roughly torn by hand

2 tablespoons fresh lemon juice

Salt to taste

Method

Gremolata: Finely chop the candied ginger and mint leaves. Combine in a bowl with the coconut. Stir to incorporate and reserve.

In a sauce pot over medium heat, add the diced red potato and cover with cold salted water. Bring the potatoes to a simmer and cook until just done, about 15 minutes. Remove the potatoes from the water and reserve in the refrigerator.

In a large pan or wok, over high heat, add the olive oil. When the oil is hot, add the red bell pepper, and sauté until slightly softened, about 2 minutes. Add the shallots and cook for 1 minute. Add the cooked potatoes and curry paste. Cook for 1 minute while incorporating the curry paste with a spoon. Add the

mussels, toss a few times, and add the white wine. Cook for 20 seconds. Add the clam juice, heavy cream and coconut milk. Stir briefly, bring to a simmer and cover. Cook for about 2 minutes. Uncover, toss in half of the torn basil, and stir. Remove the mussels, a few at a time, as the shells open and transfer to a large serving bowl. (Note: Do not overcook the mussels; a surefire sign mussels are overcooked is if they turn orange.)

Continue to cook the curry cream about 2 additional minutes to give it a little viscosity. Add the lemon juice and salt if necessary (remember the clam juice is salty).

To Serve: Toss in the last half of the torn basil and pour the sauce back over the mussels in the serving bowl. Sprinkle the gremolata generously over the top and serve immediately.

I feel I've created an inviting place where guests, whether casual or business, can enjoy exceptional food with impeccable service while feeling comfortable.

Andrew Will Winemaker Dinner
Monday, May 3, 2010

Reception

Oysters on the Half Shell; Zucchini Blossoms and Prosciutto
Crispy Veal Sweetbreads; Fava Bean Purée and Pecorino
Morel Mushroom Tartlet; Foie Pâté and Aioli

2008 Andrew Will Cab Franc Rosé

Poached Egg Salad (Bistro)

6 SERVINGS

Ingredients

Salad

¼ pound haricot vert (French green bean)

1 crusty French baguette for crostini

¼ cup olive oil

3 heads of frisee lettuce, root removed, washed and spun dry

1 bunch dandelion green or escarole, cut, washed and spun dry

2 tablespoons white wine vinegar

4 to 6 fresh eggs for poaching

Vinaigrette

½ pound good-quality thick-cut bacon, cut into ¼-inch-wide strips

1 small shallot, peeled

3 garlic cloves, peeled

¼ cup red wine vinegar

2 tablespoons chicken stock

1 teaspoon fresh thyme, chopped

1 teaspoon Dijon mustard

1 teaspoon kosher salt

½ teaspoon black pepper

¾ cup canola & olive oil blend

Method

Blanch the haricot verts by filling a saucepan with water and generously salt. Bring to a boil. When boiling, carefully drop the haricot verts in the water for about 1 minute. Remove quickly and plunge immediately into ice water to stop the cooking process. When cooled, remove the stem ends and set the beans aside. This step can be done ahead.

Crostini: Preheat the oven to 425°F. Cut the baguette crosswise in ½-inch-thick slices. Brush the slices with olive oil and place on a baking sheet. Bake until golden brown, about 10 minutes. Set aside at room temperature until ready to serve. This step can also be made in advance.

Vinaigrette: Place the bacon in a sauté pan and render over medium heat until crispy, stirring frequently. Drain the bacon fat and reserve the bacon. In a blender, add the shallot, garlic, red wine vinegar, chicken stock, thyme, mustard, salt and pepper. With the blender running on high, slowly add the canola and olive oil until the vinaigrette slightly thickens and emulsifies.

Next, fill a high-sided saucepan with water and bring to a simmer. While water is coming to a simmer, combine the frisee and dandelion leaves with the haricot vert in a large salad bowl. Add the bacon in a sauté pan and heat gently over medium-low heat. Add the vinaigrette to the pan and heat through gently. Remove immediately so the vinaigrette doesn't break.

Add the 2 tablespoons of white wine vinegar to the simmering water. This will keep the egg whites from breaking up in the water. Gently crack the eggs and drop into the water. This step may require multiple batches, depending on the quantity being served.

To Serve: Pour the warm bacon vinaigrette over the frisee and dandelion leaves and toss thoroughly. Divide the salad evenly among the plates, placing a crostini on top. Using a slotted spoon, scoop an egg out of the water and place one on top of each crostini. Season with salt and pepper.

Mixed Lettuce and Apple Salad with Candied Walnuts, Cheddar Croutons & Apple Cider Vinaigrette

4 TO 6 SERVINGS

Ingredients

Salad

2 heads Belgian endive, ends removed and leaves pulled away whole

1 head radicchio, halved, cored, and cut in 2-inch squares

1 head escarole, halved, cored, and cut in 2-inch squares

1 head frisee or curly endive, torn by hand

2 apples

1 recipe candied walnuts (see page 317)

Apple Cider Vinaigrette MAKES 1 CUP

1 quart apple cider

2 small shallots, peeled

6 garlic cloves, peeled

2 fresh thyme sprigs

½ teaspoon whole black peppercorns

1 teaspoon fresh thyme, chopped

¼ cup apple cider vinegar

½ teaspoon Dijon mustard

2 teaspoons kosher salt

½ teaspoon black pepper

¼ cup walnut oil

½ cup canola oil

Cheddar Croutons

¼ cup all-purpose flour

3 whole eggs, beaten

1½ cups fine bread crumbs

¼ pound sharp cheddar or white cheddar, cut into ½-inch squares

1 quart frying oil

Method

Apple cider vinaigrette: In a sauce pot over medium-high heat, combine the apple cider, one sliced shallot, 4 split garlic cloves, thyme sprigs and black peppercorns. Reduce the liquid down to 3 tablespoons, about 20 minutes. Strain and discard the solids. Let cool completely.

Next, add the flour in a container to dredge the cheese cubes. Do the same with the beaten egg and bread crumbs. Bread the cheese cubes in that order: flour, egg, bread crumbs. Place the cubes in a container in a single layer and place in the freezer. (Note: This can be made ahead.)

Wash the lettuces together in cold water and spin dry in a salad spinner. Keep cold until ready to serve.

As soon as the cider reduction is cool, transfer to a blender and add the other shallot, remaining garlic cloves, chopped thyme, apple cider vinegar, mustard, salt and pepper. While the blender is running, add the walnut and canola oil in a slow steady stream. Refrigerate.

Add the frying oil to a heavy-bottomed pot and bring temperature to 350°F using a candy thermometer. When the oil is up to temperature, carefully add the croutons and fry until just browned. Remove from oil and drain on paper towels.

To Serve: In a large salad bowl, toss the lettuce with a generous amount of the vinaigrette and a pinch of salt and pepper. Mix thoroughly and place even amounts of salad on each plate. Thinly slice the apple and tuck 5 or 6 slices into the lettuce. Sprinkle some of the candied walnuts over the salad and top with 5 or 6 warm croutons.

end of the haricot vert should be removed *after* blanching. The reason for this is the haricot verts are a delicate vegetable, and if the stems are removed before blanching, the beans will "drink" the water, as we like to say at the restaurant, and become soggy.)

Eggs: In a sauce pot, over medium-high heat, add the eggs, along with a pinch of salt, and cover with cold water. Like the haricot verts, have a bowl of ice water ready. Once the water reaches a simmer, cook the eggs for 9 minutes. Do not let them boil too rapidly. Remove the eggs and plunge them into the ice bath. With your thumbnail, fleck out a little piece of shell and drop back into the ice bath until cool. This will allow you to peel the eggs much easier. When the eggs are cool, gently peel them under running cool water and reserve them in the refrigerator.

Potatoes and pepper: Place the red potatoes in a small sauce pot, cover with cold water and generously salt the water. Cook the potatoes on medium heat until just tender, about 20 minutes. While the potatoes are cooking, coat the red bell pepper with a touch of oil and place on a baking sheet. Roast in the oven, rotating the pepper every couple of minutes, and cook until the skin begins to blister and turns a little brown, about 15 minutes. Remove the pepper, transfer to a small bowl, cover with plastic wrap, and place in the refrigerator. This will help steam the skin and facilitate easier peeling. When the pepper is cooled, gently remove the skin, along with the stem and innards. (Note: Do this under cool running water to help rinse away the skin, innards and, especially, the seeds. Spread the pepper out on a cutting board and julienne (thinly slice).)

Tuna: Pat the outside of the tuna loin dry and season the outer edges (not the ends) with ½ teaspoon salt and ½ teaspoon black pepper. (Note: When preparing the tuna loin, make sure the loin isn't too big, otherwise the slices placed on top of the salad will be too large.) Place a skillet large enough to hold the tuna over high-heat and add the canola oil. Bring the oil to an almost-smoking point. (Note: Make sure the kitchen fan is on.) Using a pair of kitchen tongs, gently set the tuna on one of the outer edges (not the ends). Allow the tuna to sear for about 20 seconds and quickly turn to the next edge and repeat, searing all sides (generally three or four sides), but don't sear the ends. Remove the tuna, transfer to a plate and cool in the refrigerator.

When cool, place the tuna on a cutting board and, with a very sharp knife, slice the tuna crosswise (against the grain) into ¼-inch-thick slices, about 3 to 4 slices per person.

In a soup pot over medium-high heat, add the bacon and render until crispy, about 8 minutes. Add the onion, fennel and leek, and sweat until tender and translucent. Add the tomatoes, reserved tomato juice, clam juice, wine, sachet and thyme. Bring to a boil, then reduce to a simmer. Continue to cook for 30 minutes. Add the potatoes and cook until tender. Add the clams, oregano, red wine vinegar, Old Bay seasoning, Tabasco, salt and pepper. If the soup is too chunky, feel free to add a little water to thin.

To Serve: Ladle the chowder among individual serving bowls and garnish each bowl with several clams in their shell. Serve with some rustic Italian bread.

Since the restaurant's inception, in lieu of fresh flowers on the tables, I have adorned the walls with modern Northwest art, all of which I personally select.

Yukon Potato, Fennel & Roasted Garlic

MAKES ABOUT 4 QUARTS

Ingredients

2 tablespoons unsalted butter

2 fennel bulb, tops removed, halved, cored, and cut into ¼-inch slices

1 large yellow onion, peeled, cut in half, and cut into ¼-inch slices

2¼ pound Yukon gold potatoes, peeled and diced large

2 quarts cold water

2 tablespoons salt

1 quart heavy cream

2 teaspoons ground white pepper

¼ cup herb croutons, for garnish (see page 60)

Sachet

Note: A sachet is a piece of cheesecloth filled with herbs and spices and tied off with a piece of kitchen string.

2 fresh thyme sprigs

2 bay leaves

1 tablespoon black peppercorns

1 tablespoon fennel seed

Roasted Garlic

1 cup canola oil

1 cup olive oil

3 heads of whole garlic, cloves removed and peeled

Method

In a soup pot, over medium heat, melt the butter. Add the fennel and onions and sweat the vegetables until translucent, about 8 to 10 minutes. Add the potatoes, water, sachet and salt. Cook until soft, about 30 to 35 minutes.

While the soup base is cooking, make the roasted garlic. In a separate pot over medium-low heat, add the canola oil, olive oil and the garlic cloves. Stir occasionally, cooking the garlic until lightly browned and soft, about 30 minutes. Strain the garlic from the oil and add to the soup. (Note: Cool the oil, bottle, and reserve the garlic-infused oil for future use.)

Discard the sachet, pour the soup contents into a blender and puree. While blending, add the heavy cream. (Note: It may take a couple of batches. Be careful not to overfill the blender.) Add the pepper, and check the seasoning. Add more salt if necessary.

To Serve: Ladle into individual serving bowls and garnish with herbed croutons.

Note: The oil the garlic is sautéed in is very useful for marinades, vinaigrettes or dipping for bread. We marinate our top-selling crispy chicken with the garlic-infused oil. If you don't have the time to make croutons, a little chopped parsley or chives will also work well as a garnish. You can also finish the soup with a drizzle of truffle oil.

Italian Meatball Soup

MAKES ABOUT 4 QUARTS

Ingredients

⅔ cup olive oil

1 can of diced tomatoes, drained with juice reserved

½ tablespoon kosher salt

½ teaspoon black pepper

1 large fennel bulb, diced small

1 large yellow onion, diced small

2 stalks of celery, diced small

2 tablespoons minced garlic

2 red bell peppers, diced small

6 cups chicken stock

4 cups beef stock

1 cup red wine

4 cups cannellini beans, canned, drained and rinsed

Sachet
Note: A sachet is a piece of cheesecloth filled with herbs and spices and tied off with a piece of kitchen string.

2 fresh thyme sprigs

2 bay leaves

1 tablespoon black peppercorns

Meatballs

1 tablespoon olive oil

1 tablespoon minced garlic

2 tablespoons minced shallots

1 tablespoon fresh rosemary, chopped

1¼ pound ground beef

1 whole egg

¼ cup bread crumbs

¾ tablespoon Kosher salt

½ tablespoon black pepper

Method

PREHEAT THE OVEN TO 400°F.

In a soup pot over low heat, add half of the olive oil. While the oil is heating, gently squeeze the drained tomatoes, reserving the juice, and toss them in a bowl with 1 tablespoon of olive oil, salt and pepper. Spread the tomatoes evenly on a baking sheet and place in oven for about 10 minutes. This will intensify the flavors. Remove from the oven and chop the tomatoes a little smaller.

While the tomatoes are in the oven, add the fennel, onion, celery and garlic to the warming soup pot. Cook over low heat until the vegetables are translucent. Turn the heat to high, add the bell peppers and cook until soft, about 10 to 12 minutes. Add to the vegetables the chicken and beef stocks, the sachet, red wine, tomatoes and reserved juice. Bring to a simmer, lower the heat to medium, and cook for about 40 minutes. While the soup is cooking, make the meatballs.

Meatballs: In a small sauté pan over medium heat, add 1 tablespoon of the olive oil, along with the shallots, garlic and rosemary. Cook until the shallots and are soft and translucent. Transfer to a mixing bowl, and add the ground beef, egg, bread crumbs, salt and pepper. Mix the ingredients so they are just incorporated. (Note: Do not overwork the mixture or the meatballs will be tough.) Form ¾-inch meatballs with hands. Place the meat balls, spaced apart, on a baking sheet and bake in the oven for about 7 minutes. When finished, pull them out and set aside.

To Serve: Remove the sachet from the soup, add the meatballs and beans, and cook for an additional 5 minutes to heat the beans and meatballs through. Check the seasoning and adjust with salt and pepper if necessary. Ladle the soup evenly into bowls, making sure each bowl gets an equal amount of meatballs.

Note: Often referred to as "Italian Wedding Soup," this is our version. The beans are optional, so feel free to substitute with orzo pasta or white rice. We like to garnish the soup with grated parmigiana. The meatballs can be made in advance, cooled and added during the last 10 minutes of cooking the soup.

Shrimp Bisque

MAKES 4 QUARTS

Ingredients

½ stick unsalted butter

1 small yellow onion, cut into ¼-inch-thick slices

½ leek, cut into ¼-inch-thick slices

1 small bulb fennel, cut into ¼-inch-thick slices

½ peeled carrot, cut into ¼-inch-thick slices

2 tablespoons minced garlic

¼ cup canola oil

1 pound shrimp shells

¼ cup tomato paste

10 cups water

1 cup canned diced tomatoes with juice

1 cup uncooked white rice

4 cups heavy cream

⅛ cup brandy

2 tablespoons sherry wine vinegar

⅛ cup fresh lemon juice

Kosher salt (to taste)

Fresh tarragon or parsley (for garnish)

Sachet
Note: A sachet is a piece of cheesecloth filled with herbs and spices and tied off with a piece of kitchen string.

2 sprigs of fresh thyme

2 bay leaves

1 tablespoon black peppercorns

Method

In a large pot over low heat, melt the butter and sweat the onion, leek, fennel, carrot and garlic until soft. While the vegetables are cooking, heat the canola oil in a separate pan and add the shrimp shells. Saute the shells until they turn red. Add the shells and tomato paste to the sweated vegetables. Raise the heat to medium-high, and cook for 2 minutes, stirring frequently.

Next, add the water, tomatoes and their juice, rice and herb sachet. Bring to a simmer and cook for 45 minutes. Remove from heat, and remove the sachet. Add the cream and transfer to a blender. Blend the contents, including the

Sandwiches

Four-Cheese Quiche

Ingredients

Quiche Dough

2½ cups all-purpose flour, sifted

1 teaspoon kosher salt

10 ounces unsalted butter, cut into cubes and chilled

2 tablespoons water

Canola oil, as needed

2 pounds dried white beans (to help retain quiche shell when cooking)

Quiche Filling

8 whole eggs

1½ cups heavy cream

1½ cups whole milk

1 tablespoon kosher salt

1 teaspoon black pepper

4 ounces grated medium cheddar

4 ounces grated Gruyere

2 ounces finely grated parmigiana

2 ounces shredded mozzarella

Method

Quiche dough: Add half of the sifted flour and the salt into a fitted bowl of a standing mixer (or hand mixer). Using the paddle attachment, turn the mixer on low and add the butter, a few cubes at a time. When the last of the butter is added, turn up the speed slightly to make sure the butter is completely mixed in. Return the speed to low and add the rest of the flour. Make sure the additional flour is combined and add the water. Mix until the dough feels smooth to the touch and there are no visible chunks of butter. Pat the dough into a disk about 8 inches in diameter, wrap in plastic, and refrigerate for at least two hours.

Place a piece of parchment paper on a baking sheet. Lightly brush a 9-inch by 2-inch-high ring mold with canola oil and place the ring on the baking sheet. Remove the chilled dough from the refrigerator, place on a floured work surface, pat some more flour over the dough, and make a slightly larger round. Then, using a rolling pin, roll out the dough to about $\frac{1}{16}$ inch thick and 14 inches in diameter. Roll the dough on to the pin so it curls around it, and gently and evenly place the dough into the ring mold. Be sure to carefully push the dough down to the bottom and into the edges, being careful not to tear the dough. (Note: There will be 1 inch or more of excess, which is a good thing). Trim off any dough in excess of 1 inch and reserve the scraps for possible future patchwork. Next, fold the 1 inch of excess dough over the edges. This will keep the dough from shrinking too much as it bakes. Check for any cracks or tears and use the scraps to patch them up if necessary. Place the baking sheet with the pie shell into the refrigerator for 30 minutes to cool.

Preheat the oven to 400°F. Place a rack in the center of the oven. Remove the baking sheet with tart shell from the refrigerator and place a piece of parchment inside the shell. Fill the shell to the top with the dried beans. Place the shell in the oven and bake until the edges and bottom are lightly brown, about 25 minutes. Remove the beans and parchment paper, and continue baking until the edges and bottom are golden brown, about 10 minutes. Remove and cool completely at room temperature. When cool, check for any cracks and patch if necessary.

Quiche filling: Preheat the oven to 325°F. In a mixing bowl, add the eggs, cream, milk, salt and pepper. Whisk vigorously until the mixture becomes frothy, which may take several minutes. (Note: A blender also works well for this procedure, and will make the quiche lighter.) Next, mix the cheeses together and spread half of the cheese evenly on the bottom of the quiche shell. Transfer the wet ingredients to a pitcher or similar container and carefully pour the ingredients into the shell to the halfway point. Add the rest of the cheese. Place the tart shell in the oven, on the baking sheet, and carefully fill the tart with the wet ingredients, careful not to spill over the edges. Bake uncovered for about 1½ hours, or until the top is lightly brown and the center doesn't jiggle. Remove the tart and cool to room temperature. Using a sharp knife or small metal spatula, carefully scrape the excess dough from the edges so there isn't any dough hanging over the edge. Refrigerate the tarts for several hours, or up to a couple of days.

To Serve: Preheat the oven to 350°F. Remove the cooled quiche from the refrigerator, and, using a tip of a knife, run the knife around the edges to loosen the quiche. Carefully lift the ring mold off, and slice the quiche into the desired number of pieces. Place on a baking sheet and place in the oven for 10 to 12 minutes, or until warmed through.

Note: This is a basic four-cheese quiche recipe. You can use any kind of fillings: bacon, mushrooms, onions, roasted peppers, fresh herbs or other cheeses. Just be careful the ingredients do not have too much water in them, as this will upset the custard as it cooks.

Method

Balsamic onions: Preheat the oven to 400°F. In a large sauté pan, over high heat, add the olive oil. When hot, add the red onion rings and cook until they get a little color, stirring occasionally. Add the salt, pepper, and balsamic vinegar. Bring to a simmer and transfer to a small roasting pan. Cover with foil and place in the oven. Cook until the onions are soft and dark in color, about 20 minutes. Remove from oven and let cool.

Harissa mayonnaise: In a food processor, add the egg, caraway seed, coriander seed, chili powder, salt, pepper, tomato paste, lemon juice and garlic. While the machine is running, add the canola and olive oil in a slow, steady stream. Check the seasoning. Refrigerate.

Polenta fries: In a heavy-bottomed pot, add the frying oil, and heat over medium-high heat. Dredge the polenta "fries" in the semolina flour, shake off excess, and fry until crispy, about 3 to 4 minutes. Remove from the oil and drain on paper towels. Sprinkle with salt and place them on a baking sheet. Keep warm in oven until ready to serve.

Lamb burgers: In a large mixing bowl, combine the lamb, red pepper flakes, shallots, garlic, cumin, rosemary, salt and pepper. Mix well. Form 4 burgers (about 8 ounces each) and refrigerate.

Turn on an outdoor grill to high heat. While grill is heating, season the lamb burgers with salt and pepper and place on the grill. Cook for 8 minutes, turning once during cooking. Top each burger with some of the caramelized red onions. Grill for 1 additional minute. Brush the burger buns with extra virgin olive oil and lightly grill them.

To Serve: Spread a generous amount of the harissa mayonnaise on each bun half and top with some fresh arugula leaves. Place the burger with onions on the buns, add a side of the polenta fries and serve.

Note: Harissa is a standard sauce or condiment in North African cuisine. It is a great match for the gaminess of ground lamb. We have westernized the sauce in America by turning it into a mayonnaise.

Royal's
Steak Sandwich

Ingredients

2½ pounds thinly sliced top sirloin or skirt steak

4 tablespoons olive oil

Salt and pepper, to taste

2 yellow onions, peeled and julienned (thinly sliced)

2 red bell peppers, julienned

1 yellow bell pepper, julienned

4 jalapeno, thinly sliced

4 tablespoons chopped garlic

3 tablespoons red pepper flakes

¾ cup heavy cream

4 cups pepper jack cheese, shredded

6 crusty baguettes

Method

PREHEAT THE OVEN TO 450°F.

Tenderize the slices of meat by laying them out on a cutting board. Place a piece of plastic wrap over the meat and, using a kitchen mallet, pound the meat thin, about ¼ inch thick. Using 2 large sauté pans over high heat, add 1½ tablespoons of olive oil to each pan. Season the meat with salt and pepper. Bring the oil to a smoking point. Divide the meat evenly between the two pans to ensure a hard sear.

In a third pan over high heat, bring the last tablespoon of oil to the smoking point. Add the onions, peppers and jalapenos. Toss frequently and sauté them until lightly caramelized, about 8 minutes.

Continue cooking the meat over high heat until it begins to brown. Add the sautéed onions, peppers and jalapenos. Add the chopped garlic and chili flakes, and sauté 2 additional minutes. Deglaze the pan with the heavy cream,

Sauces & Stocks

Chitchen Stock

MAKES 1½ GALLONS

Ingredients

2 gallons cold water

5 pounds chicken bones (wings, feet, body, necks and backs are all acceptable)

2 carrots, large chop

2 celery stalks, large chop

2 yellow onions, large chop

2 leek, large chop

6 garlic cloves, peeled and halved

3 bay leaves

1 tablespoon black peppercorns

1 tablespoon mustard seed

2 cups white wine

½ bunch parsley stems

Method

In a large stock pot over high heat, combine the cold water, chicken bones, carrots, celery, onion, leek, garlic, bay leaves, pepper, mustard seed, white wine and parsley. Bring to a boil, then turn down heat and simmer for 4 to 6 hours, skimming impurities that periodically rise to the surface. Add more cold water as necessary to keep the bones covered. Strain and cool. Freeze and store excess.

Note: When making protein-based stocks, cold water is of the utmost importance. Hot or warm water will cause stocks to become overly cloudy and will not properly release the impurities that must be skimmed off. Skimming is crucial in developing a clear and flavorful stock. The stock can be frozen up to several months.

Rich Poultry Jus

MAKES ABOUT 6 CUPS

Ingredients

2 tablespoons canola oil

1 small yellow onion, roughly chopped

1 carrot, roughly chopped

1 leek, roughly chopped

1 celery stalk, roughly chopped

6 garlic cloves, peeled and halved

½ cup red wine vinegar

1 cup red wine

1 teaspoon fennel seed

1 teaspoon coriander seed

3 quarts chicken stock

3 fresh thyme sprigs

Method

Add the canola oil to a large saucepan, over high heat. Add the onion, carrot, leek, celery and garlic. Stir occasionally and cook until vegetables are nicely brown and caramelized. Add the red wine vinegar and cook until the vinegar has evaporated. Add the red wine and reduce by half. Add the fennel seed, coriander seed, chicken stock and thyme sprigs, and reduce the heat to medium. Let simmer and reduce by half. Strain and cool.

Note: When you remove a roasted chicken out of the oven, pour a couple ladles of this poultry jus in the pan, scrape up the bits on the bottom, and finish it with a little butter.

Mushroom Stock

MAKES 4 QUARTS

Ingredients

6 quarts cold water

1 small yellow onion, roughly chopped

1 carrot, roughly chopped

1 small fennel bulb, roughly chopped

1 celery stalk, roughly chopped

1 leek, roughly chopped

6 garlic cloves, peeled and split

¼ cup dried porcini mushrooms
(or other dried mushrooms)

2 cups fresh, assorted mushroom stems, or mushrooms, roughly chopped

2 bay leaves

½ tablespoon black peppercorns

½ tablespoon mustard seeds

2 fresh thyme sprigs

¼ cup white wine

Method

In a large stock pot over high heat, add the water, onion, carrot, fennel, celery, leek, garlic, dried mushrooms, mushroom stems, bay leaves, peppercorns, mustard seeds, thyme sprigs and white wine. Bring to a boil, then reduce heat to medium. Let simmer for 1 hour. Strain and cool.

Soy Ginger Glaze

YIELDS ABOUT 2½ CUPS

Ingredients

2 cups soy sauce

1 cup brown sugar

1 tablespoon rice wine vinegar

¼ cup cream sherry

¾ cup orange juice

⅛ cup fresh lime juice

1 knob ginger root, peeled and roughly chopped

1 shallot, peeled and roughly chopped

1 tablespoon cornstarch

1 tablespoon water

Method

In a stock pot, over medium-high heat, combine the soy sauce, brown sugar, rice wine vinegar, cream sherry, orange juice, lime juice, ginger and shallot. Stir occasionally to keep the shallots and ginger from scorching the bottom. When the mixture comes to a boil, remove from the heat and allow the mixture to steep, about 15 minutes.

Bring the liquid back to a boil over medium-high heat. Meanwhile, combine the cornstarch and water in a small dish, stirring with a small spoon until the cornstarch completely dissolves and forms a slurry. When the liquid comes to a boil, whisk in the cornstarch slurry. The liquid should begin to thicken. Allow the mixture to boil for another minute, remove from the heat, and strain through a fine-mesh strainer. Cool and store. (Note: This sauce will thicken a little more after it is cooled.) This glaze is meant to be served cold.

Note: This sauce has a wide variety of uses. It can be served as a dipping sauce with ahi tuna or it can be used to glaze fish. The glaze also works well as a marinade or with vinaigrettes. The glaze will hold for a couple months in the refrigerator.

Shrimp Stock

Ingredients

3 tablespoons canola oil

1 pound shrimp shells (heads and tails acceptable)

1 carrot, roughly chopped

1 small yellow onion, roughly chopped

1 celery stalk, roughly chopped

1 leek, roughly chopped

2 Roma tomatoes, quartered

2 tablespoons tomato paste

¼ cup brandy

2 bay leaves

6 parsley stems

½ tablespoon coriander seeds

½ tablespoon mustard seeds

½ tablespoon black peppercorns

6 quarts cold water

Method

Add the canola oil to a stockpot over high heat. Add the shrimp shells, stirring frequently. Cook the shells until they turn bright orange. Add the carrot, onion, celery, leek and Roma tomatoes. Stir frequently, cooking the vegetables until they become slightly softened. Add the tomato paste. Continue stirring to allow tomato paste to evenly coat the vegetables and shrimp shells. Continue cooking until the tomato paste starts to dry, but does not burn. Add the brandy and scrape any bits that may have caramelized on the bottom of the pan. Add the bay leaves, parsley stems, coriander seeds, mustard seeds, peppercorns and water. Bring to a boil and reduce heat to a simmer. Let simmer for 2 hours. Strain and cool.

Citrus "House" Vinaigrette

MAKES 1 CUP

Ingredients

¼ cup fresh-squeezed lemon juice

½ teaspoon Dijon mustard

¾ cup olive oil

Salt and pepper, to taste

Method

Add the lemon juice and mustard in a small bowl. While whisking, add the oil in a slow, steady stream. Season with salt and pepper.

Vin Blanc

Ingredients

½ small yellow onion, roughly chopped

½ carrot, roughly chopped

½ leek, roughly chopped

½ celery stalk, roughly chopped

4 garlic cloves, peeled and split

½ cup white wine vinegar

2 cups white wine

1½ cups chicken stock

2 bay leaves

½ tablespoon white peppercorns

½ tablespoon mustard seeds

6 cups heavy cream

Method

In a large saucepan, add the onion, carrot, leek, celery, garlic and white wine vinegar. Turn the heat on high, and reduce vinegar until almost dry. Add the white wine and reduce it by half. Add the chicken stock, bay leaves, peppercorns and mustard seeds. Bring to a simmer. Add the heavy cream, bring to a simmer, then turn the heat to medium-low and allow to simmer gently for about 20 minutes. Strain, refrigerate and cool.

Note: This is one of the more versatile French sauces. Vin blanc can be flavored with a variety of herbs, mushrooms or different-flavored vinegars. Vin blanc goes well with fish, and mussels or clams can also be steamed in the sauce.

1-Day Creme Fraiche

MAKES 1¼ CUPS

Ingredients

1 teaspoon fresh lemon juice

1 cup heavy cream

¼ cup buttermilk

1 teaspoon kosher salt

Method

Using a clean, dry plastic container with a lid, add the lemon juice and shake the container vigorously so the lemon juice coats the interior of the container. Add the heavy cream and buttermilk. Stir briefly, then carefully sprinkle the salt over the top of the mixture. Do not mix in. Place the lid back on and store at room temperature for 24 hours.

When ready, the mixture should be noticeably thicker. Store in the refrigerator and allow to completely cool before using. Once cool, the creme fraiche can be whipped to thicken or left in a runnier state. This creme fraiche will hold up well for a couple weeks in the refrigerator.

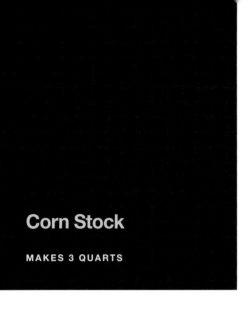

Corn Stock

MAKES 3 QUARTS

Ingredients

1 small yellow onion, roughly chopped

1 peeled carrot, roughly chopped

1 fennel bulb, roughly chopped

1 celery stalk, roughly chopped

1 leek, roughly chopped

6 cloves garlic, peeled and halved

6 white mushrooms, halved

2 bay leaves

½ tablespoon coriander seeds

½ tablespoon fennel seeds

½ tablespoon mustard seeds

6 ears of sweet yellow corn, shucked and kernels scraped off

1 gallon cold water

3 basil stems

Method

In a large stockpot, add the onion, carrot, fennel, celery, leek, garlic, mush-rooms, bay leaves, coriander seeds, fennel seeds and mustard seeds. Using the back of a knife, scrape each cob to force some of the milk into the stock pot. Break the cobs in half and add to the pot. Fill the pot with the cold water and, over high heat, bring the stock to a boil. When boiling, turn down to medium and simmer for about 1 hour. Add the basil stems and simmer for an additional 10 minutes. Strain and cool.

Note: Corn stock may seem a little odd, but in the summertime, we find the stock indispensable. We use the corn stock to make risottos, soups and sauces. This stock can spoil rather quickly, so if you don't use it all immedi-ately, freeze it.

Ingredients

4 cups olive oil

2 tablespoons minced garlic

1 tablespoon dried Italian seasoning

¼ tablespoon kosher salt

¼ teaspoon black pepper

2 tablespoons chopped fresh Italian parsley

Method

In a sauce pot over medium-high heat, add the oil and garlic. Cook until the garlic just begins to brown. Remove the garlic from the heat and add the Italian seasoning, salt, pepper and parsley. Cool and refrigerate.

To Serve: Serve alongside bread as you would with butter.

Ricotta Gnocchi with English Peas, Fava Beans & Lemon Cream

4 TO 6 SERVINGS

Ingredients

½ cup fresh-shelled English peas

1 teaspoon olive oil

2 pounds fava beans

1 recipe vin blanc (see page 150)

1 pound fresh ricotta cheese, excess moisture squeezed out or drained

2 tablespoons finely grated parmigiana

1 cup all-purpose flour, sifted

1 egg

2 teaspoons kosher salt

1 lemon, zested and juiced

½ teaspoon grated nutmeg

1 cup diced heirloom tomatoes or grape tomatoes cut in half

1 tablespoon fresh Italian parsley, washed and chopped

½ teaspoon black pepper

Method

Bring a small, generously salted pot of water to a boil. Set up a small bowl of ice water on the side to cool the vegetables. Blanch the peas by carefully adding them to the boiling water, for 45 seconds. Remove the peas and plunge them into the ice water. When cool, remove from the ice bath. Toss with the olive oil, and set aside. Next, remove the fava beans from the large pod. Carefully add the favas to the boiling water. As soon as they float to the surface they are done. Quickly remove them and plunge into the ice water. When cool remove the "second skin" by scraping a small hole on each one, gently squeezing them out. The favas will be vibrant green. Discard any drab, yellow-colored favas. This step can be done ahead of time.

Make the vin blanc recipe by following page 150.

Gnocchi: In a fitted bowl of a standing mixer, using the dough-hook attachment, combine the ricotta and parmigiana cheeses, 1 cup of the flour, the egg, salt, lemon zest and nutmeg. Start mixer on low and, when the flour is partially incorporated, increase to medium. Mix until the ingredients are just incorporated. Do not overwork the dough; it should feel somewhat tacky.

Transfer the dough to a floured work surface. Pat the dough with a little flour and portion the dough into 4 equal-sized balls. Roll each ball into a long ½-inch-diameter rope. If the dough sticks to the table at any point, just sprinkle a touch more flour.

Before cutting the gnocchi, fill a large pot (preferably with a colander) with salted water over high heat.

Once the ropes are rolled out, using a pastry scraper or knife, cut the gnocchi on a slight bias and about ½ inch wide. Set up large bowl of ice water. Using a large spatula, carefully transfer the gnocchi to the pot of simmering water. Allow the gnocchi to float to the top. When at the top, cook for 30 additional seconds. Quickly remove the gnocchi and plunge them into the ice bath to cool. Toss the cooled gnocchi with the olive oil, and reserve in refrigerator.

Using a large sauté pan over high heat, add the vin blanc and bring to a simmer. Add the gnocchi. (Note: It is okay to crowd the pan, but don't let the gnocchi mound up.) Toss several times, coating the gnocchi with the vin blanc sauce. Add the peas, fava beans and tomatoes. Toss a couple more times. Add the chopped parsley and lemon juice. Season with salt and pepper.

To Serve: Serve in individual bowls, ladling any of the remaining sauce over the top.

Sweet Potato Gnocchi with Cashews, Pancetta, Cippolini Onions & Maple-Brown Butter

4 SERVINGS

Ingredients

1⅓ pounds sweet potato

2 teaspoons olive oil

¼ pound pancetta, cut into 1-inch-long by ¼-inch-wide lardons

½ pound cippolini onions, peeled and quartered

½ teaspoon black pepper

1¼ cup all-purpose flour, sifted

1 tablespoon brown sugar

1 whole egg

¼ pound unsalted butter

⅓ cups salt-roasted cashews, roughly chopped

2 tablespoons maple syrup

2 teaspoons fresh sage, chopped

2 tablespoons kosher salt

1½ tablespoon grated parmigiana

Method

In a large pot of lightly salted cold water over medium heat, add the sweet potatoes. Cook until just tender, about 40 minutes.

Preheat the oven to 400°F.

In a sauté pan over medium heat, add 1 teaspoon of olive oil. When hot, add the pancetta lardons. Stir frequently, and render until almost crispy, about 12 minutes. Remove the pancetta and reserve. In a small bowl, toss the cippolini onions with the pancetta fat and dash of black pepper. Place the onions on a parchment-lined baking sheet and roast until golden brown, about 15 minutes. Set aside.

Gnocchi: Add the potatoes to a pot of lightly salted cold water. Cook on medium until the potatoes are just tender, about 40 minutes. Remove from

heat. When the potatoes are cool enough to handle, remove the skin. Lightly flour a work surface. Place the potatoes in a food mill or potato ricer and rice the potato onto the work surface. Create a well in the center of the potatoes and cover the potato and some of the center with 1 cup of the flour and the brown sugar. Crack the egg in the center. With a fork, lightly beat the egg and begin drawing the potato and flour in, towards the center. When the fork becomes useless, fold the dough with your hands, first making sure to get the ingredients incorporated and then fold it over itself a few times. Do not knead or overwork the dough. The dough should feel fairly dry. Pat the dough with a little flour and portion the dough into 6 equal-sized balls. Roll each ball into a long ½-inch diameter rope. If the dough sticks to the table at any point just sprinkle a touch more flour.

Before cutting the gnocchi, fill a large pot (preferably with a colander) with salted water over high heat.

Once the ropes are rolled out, using a pastry scraper or knife, cut the gnocchi on a slight bias and about ½-inch wide. Set up large bowl of ice water. Using a large spatula, carefully transfer the gnocchi to the pot of simmering water. Allow the gnocchi to float to the top. When at the top, cook for 30 additional seconds. Quickly remove the gnocchi and plunge them into the ice bath to cool. Toss the cooled gnocchi with a little olive oil & reserve in refrigerator.

Using a large sauté pan over high heat, add the butter and let foam. Add the gnocchi. (Note: It is okay to crowd the pan, but don't let the gnocchi mound up.) Toss several times. When the butter slightly browns, add the pancetta, cippolini onions and cashews. Toss a couple more times, and add the maple syrup and sage. Season with salt and pepper.

To Serve: Divide the gnocchi among individual serving bowls, and ladle the remaining butter over the top. Sprinkle with grated parmigiana and serve.

Golden Potato Gnocchi with Asparagus, Ramps & Basil Beurre Blanc

4 TO 6 SERVINGS

Ingredients

1 bunch asparagus, remove the bottom 2 inches and discard

1 pound wild ramps

1⅓ pounds Yukon gold potatoes

1 cup all-purpose flour, sifted

1 whole egg

½ pound unsalted butter, room temperature, cut into cubes

⅛ cup white wine

2 tablespoons heavy cream

2 tablespoons basil, thinly sliced

1 tablespoon fresh lemon juice

3 teaspoons kosher salt

½ teaspoon black pepper

Method

Bring a pot of generously salted water to a boil. When boiling, add the asparagus and blanch for 2 minutes. Remove the asparagus and immediately plunge into a bowl of ice water. Cool completely. When cool, remove the asparagus and cut into 1-inch pieces. Refrigerate.

Rinse the ramps under cold water and, with a paring knife, trim any brown root off the end. Remove the green leaves and reserve. Remove the white part of the ramp as well, cut into 1-inch lengths and reserve.

Gnocchi: Add the potatoes to a pot of lightly salted cold water. Cook on medium until the potatoes are just tender, about 40 minutes. Remove from heat. When the potatoes are cool enough to handle, remove the skin. Lightly flour a work surface. Place the potatoes in a food mill or potato ricer and rice the potato onto the work surface. Create a well in the center of the potatoes

Fish & Shellfish

Crab Cakes with Corn Salsa & Avocado Sauce

**6 SERVINGS (MAKES 24
2½ OUNCES CRAB CAKES)**

Ingredients

Crab Cakes

⅔ cup heavy cream

¾ teaspoons ground white pepper

1 teaspoon cayenne pepper

2 tablespoons canola oil

½ small yellow onion, peeled and
very finely diced

½ yellow bell pepper, seeded and
very finely diced

1 red bell pepper, very finely diced

2 cups panko (Japanese bread crumbs)

2 cups bread crumbs

2 pounds fresh Dungeness crab meat,
thoroughly drained

3 eggs

½ bunch Italian flat-leaf parsley, washed
and finely chopped

2 tablespoons chervil, finely chopped

2 tablespoons chives, finely chopped

2 tablespoons tarragon, finely chopped

6 cups frying oil

Avocado Sauce

1 teaspoon minced garlic

2 ripe avocados, peeled and pitted

2 eggs

2 teaspoons Dijon mustard

2 teaspoons lime juice

2 teaspoons lemon juice

1 teaspoon cayenne pepper

2 teaspoons kosher salt

½ teaspoon black pepper

2 cups canola oil

Corn Salsa MAKES ABOUT 1 QUART

2 cups corn kernels, fresh, frozen or canned

1 red bell pepper, roasted, seeded, peeled
and small diced

½ red onion, peeled and small diced

3 tablespoons chopped fresh cilantro

1 finely minced jalapeno

1 tablespoon kosher salt

½ teaspoon black pepper

Juice of 1 lemon

Method

Crab cakes: In a saucepan over low heat, combine the heavy cream, white pepper and cayenne pepper. Whisk occasionally and allow the mixture to cook and slightly thicken, about 15 minutes. Cool the mixture.

In a small sauté pan, over medium-high heat, add 2 teaspoons of canola oil, and sauté onions until translucent, about 3 minutes. Transfer the onions to a small bowl, wipe the pan out with a paper towel and 2 more teaspoons of the canola oil. Repeat the process with the yellow bell peppers and red bell peppers. Cool the vegetables.

Add the panko to a food processor and run for 20 seconds. Pulse in all but 2 tablespoons of the bread crumbs and transfer the breading to a container that will allow the cakes to be breaded in. Set aside.

Once the vegetables are cool, add the cooled cream and combine thoroughly. Add the remaining 2 tablespoons of bread crumbs, crab meat, 3 eggs, and the chopped parsley, chervil, chives and tarragon. Mix until the ingredients are just incorporated, trying not to break up the larger lumps.

Pre-portion the mixture (an ice cream scoop works well for this) and gently form the cake into a slightly flattened ball. Do not squeeze or press too hard. Set the cake right into the breading, pile some of the breading on top so the cake is buried. Pick the cake up and gently re-form the cake into a slightly flattened round, being sure to round the edges. Sprinkle more breading on as necessary, but don't pack too tightly or the cakes will become dry. Refrigerate.

Avocado sauce: In a food processor, combine the garlic, avocados, eggs, mustard, lime juice, lemon juice, cayenne pepper, salt and pepper. While the machine is running, add the canola oil in steady stream. Refrigerate.

Corn salsa: In a mixing bowl, combine the corn, red bell pepper, red onion, cilantro, jalapeno, salt, pepper and lemon juice. Chill until ready to serve.

In a heavy-bottomed pan, over medium-high heat, add the frying oil and bring to 350°F. (use a candy thermometer). Add the crab cakes in, careful not to crowd them, and cook until golden brown. Turn them over once during cooking. Transfer to paper towels.

To Serve: Spread the avocado sauce on each of six dinner plates, starting in the center and working outwards in a circular motion. Place some of the corn salsa in the middle of the plate. Lean four of the crab cakes against the salsa, and garnish with a sprig of fresh cilantro.

Note: Crab cakes make great hors d'ouevres! Just make them smaller when serving as an appetizer.

Copper River King Salmon with Butternut Squash Croquettes, Braised Red Cabbage & Sauce Beurre Rouge

4 SERVINGS

Ingredients

Croquettes
1 butternut squash, peeled, seeded, and cut in 1-inch cubes

4 large eggs

1½ cups all-purpose flour

3 cups panko (Japanese bread crumbs)

1 tablespoon salt

1 teaspoon allspice

1 teaspoon black pepper

2 quarts canola oil

Salmon
1 recipe braised red cabbage (see page 288)

1 shallot, peeled and thinly sliced

1 sprig fresh thyme

⅛ cup red wine vinegar

¼ cup pinot noir (red wine)

4 Copper River king salmon fillets (6 ounces each), center cut, skin on, pinbones removed.

2 tablespoons olive oil

1½ tablespoon kosher salt

½ teaspoon black pepper

1 tablespoon heavy cream

½ pound unsalted butter, cut into cubes, room temperature

Method

Croquettes: Using a double boiler or wok steamer, steam the butternut squash until it is fork tender, about 45 minutes. Place the squash on a towel-lined baking sheet and allow to partially cool and dry, about 15 minutes. Transfer the cooked squash to the fitted bowl of a standing mixer (or hand mixer). Turn the mixer on medium with the whisk attachment running, and add 1 egg, ½ cup flour, 1 cup panko, salt, allspice and black pepper. Mix until the ingredients are incorporated. Spread the mixture on a baking sheet and cool for 1 hour.

Make an egg wash using the remaining 3 eggs and ¼ cup water. Whisk together and pour in a soup bowl. Pour the remaining flour in a similar bowl, and the remaining panko in another.

With hands, form the butternut mixture into small egg-shapes, about 1½ inches long (this should make 18 to 20 croquettes). Using one hand for the wet ingredients and one for the dry, dip and roll the croquettes in the following order: flour, egg, panko. Coat them well. As each one is finished, place on a parchment-lined baking sheet and reserve until ready to fry.

Preheat the oven to 350°F.

Pour the frying oil into a dry, heavy-bottomed pot. Turn the heat to medium-high, reaching a temperature of 350°F (use a candy thermometer). Add half of the croquettes in the oil and fry until golden brown and crispy. Transfer to paper towels and fry the other half. Once the excess oil has been dried off, transfer the croquettes to a baking sheet. Set aside at room temperature.

Place the braised cabbage in a sauté pan and gently warm.

Begin reducing the sauce: In another small sauce pot over medium-low, add the sliced shallot, thyme, red wine vinegar and red wine. Let reduce down to 2 tablespoons.

Next, pat the salmon dry and season the flesh side with salt and pepper. In a large nonstick skillet on medium-high, add the olive oil. When hot, set the pieces of salmon in flesh side down. Sear until golden brown, about 2 to 3 minutes. Turn the salmon over and cook the skin side down until crispy and lightly brown, about 5 minutes.

Place the croquettes in the oven to keep warm.

Once the wine and vinegar have reduced, and with the heat turned to very low, add the cream. Let bubble briefly, then begin whisking in the butter a few chunks at a time until all the butter is added and the sauce is a velvety, creamy red. Remove the pan from the heat just before the last piece of butter has melted. Make sure to whisk or swirl the pan the entire time. Remove the shallots and thyme. Season with salt.

To Serve: Place a small mound of the cabbage (using a slotted spoon to drain excess liquid) in the center of each plate. Spoon a couple tablespoons of the sauce around the cabbage. Place a croquette at each of three points on the plate and set a piece of salmon, skin side down, on top of the cabbage.

Alaskan Halibut with Baby Artichokes, Heirloom Tomatoes & Creamy Basil Sauce

6 SERVINGS

Ingredients

Baby artichokes

12 baby artichokes (or 4 large chokes)

1 lemon

1 bunch fresh thyme (tied with butcher's twine)

2 bay leaves

2 quarts chicken stock

½ cup white wine

2 tablespoons extra virgin olive oil

1 teaspoon salt

Basil Sauce MAKES 1 CUP

1 shallot, peeled

2 garlic cloves, peeled

1 cup fresh basil leaves, packed

¼ cup white wine vinegar

½ tablespoon fresh lemon juice

1 teaspoon Dijon mustard

2 teaspoons Kosher salt

½ teaspoon black pepper

¾ cup olive oil

Halibut

6 Alaskan halibut fillets (6 ounces each), skin off, center cut, bone out

3 tablespoons olive oil

½ teaspoon kosher salt

½ teaspoon black pepper

2 large heirloom tomatoes, multiple colors, sliced into thin rounds

¼ cup fresh Italian parsley leaves

¼ cup fresh fennel fronds

¼ cup fresh tarragon leaves

1 tablespoon house vinaigrette (see page 149)

Method

Artichokes: Gently peel away the first couple of outer green layers of leaves until the inside is yellow with a few green tips. With a sharp paring knife, remove the top ⅛ inch of the artichoke. Turn the choke upside down and remove the brown end from the stem. In an upward peeling motion, trim the stem up to the leaves all the way around (removing any green from the stem without removing the entire stem). Cut the artichoke in half lengthwise and, with the tip of the knife, trim away any sharp points inside the choke.

Preheat the oven to 350°F.

With a sharp peeler, peel the lemon, trying to get as little of the pith as possible. Thinly slice the pieces of lemon peel and reserve. Cut the lemon in half, juice (no seeds) and reserve.

In an ovenproof sauce pot over medium-high heat, add the chokes, thyme, bay leaves, stock, wine and reserved lemon juice. Bring to a simmer, then cover with a lid or foil. Transfer to the oven and braise for 40 minutes, or until the chokes are tender. Remove the chokes, toss with the lemon zest, olive oil and salt. Allow to cool. Refrigerate.

Basil sauce: In a blender, add the shallot, garlic, basil, white wine vinegar, lemon juice, mustard, salt and pepper. Turn on high and, while the blender is running, add the olive oil in a slow, steady stream. Refrigerate until ready to use. Stores 3 to 5 days.

Remove the baby artichokes from the refrigerator and bring up to room temperature.

Preheat the oven to 425°F.

Turn an outdoor grill to medium-high heat. Pat the halibut fillets dry with paper towels. Brush the tops (flesh side) with olive oil and season with salt and pepper.

Make sure the grill grates are oiled or sprayed with nonstick grill. When hot, place the halibut seasoned side down. Allow the halibut to cook untouched for about 4 minutes then turn three-quarters to create crosshatch marks while cooking for an additional 3 to 4 minutes. Remove the halibut from the grill and transfer, grill marks facing up, to a baking sheet. Brush the halibut with a little more olive oil, and place in the oven to finish, about 4 minutes.

While the halibut is finishing, place the baby artichokes face down on the grill and cook for 1 minute. Turn over and cook an additional minute. Remove from heat.

To Serve: Arrange the heirloom tomato slices in an overlapping spiral in the center of each plate, leaving a small hole in the center for the artichokes. Season the tomatoes with salt and pepper. Drizzle some of the basil sauce around the tomatoes. Arrange 4 pieces of artichoke in the center of each plate and place a piece of halibut on top of the artichokes. In a small bowl, toss the parsley, fennel and tarragon with some of the house vinaigrette and gently place a small amount of herb salad on each halibut.

Note: Baby artichokes, when you can find them, are the recommended choice, but substituting larger chokes are equally delicious. When it comes to cleaning the larger chokes, however, the process is slightly different. After you remove the green outer leaves, you actually want to remove the remaining leaves. Hold the choke by the stem sideways on a cutting board just above where the heart is, and cut straight through. Trim the stem the same way, but remove some of the bottom if the stem is too long. Once the stem is trimmed, cut it in half lengthwise, remove the spiny "choke" needles, then cut the two halves in half again. Cook the large chokes the same way. I also highly recommend using latex gloves while working with raw artichokes because the chokes leave an extremely bitter flavor on everything and they will severely oxidize your skin.

Curried Halibut Cheeks with Red & Golden Beets, Ruby Red Grapefruit & Dill Emulsion

4 TO 6 SERVINGS

Ingredients

½ pound red beets

½ pound golden beets

1 cup extra virgin olive oil

1½ tablespoon kosher salt

1½ teaspoon black pepper

1 pound rock salt

2 ruby red grapefruit

¼ cup rice wine vinegar

½ teaspoon Dijon mustard

2 tablespoons finely minced shallot

2 tablespoons finely chopped baby dill

2 pounds fresh halibut cheeks

¼ cup yellow curry powder

Method

PREHEAT THE OVEN TO 425°F.

Beets: Toss the beets with 2 tablespoons of olive oil, ½ tablespoons of salt, and ½ teaspoon of black pepper. Place the rock salt on a baking sheet, loosely wrap the beets individually in foil and place them on the rock salt and into the oven. Roast until just tender. Depending on the size, about 45 minutes. Check the beets by piercing them with a bamboo skewer. If the skewer sinks in with a slight amount of resistance, they are done. Remove and cool before peeling.

Once the beets are cool, use a kitchen towel or paper towel (rubber gloves work well too) and rub the skins off. Be sure to peel the golden beets first because the red beets will bleed over everything. Once the golden beets are peeled, use a vegetable slicer or mandolin to slice (note: if the beets are too large, cut them in half). Thinly slice the beets. Set them aside and repeat with the red beets.

Vinaigrette: remove the ends from the grapefruit and remove the rind down to the flesh. Section the grapefruit and collect the juice. Reserve the sections and strain the juice into a small saucepan. Over medium heat, reduce the juice by half. Cool the juice. In a mixing bowl, combine the juice, the rice wine vinegar, ½ teaspoon salt, ½ teaspoon black pepper, and the mustard. While whisking, add ⅔ of the oil in a slow steady stream. Stir in the shallots, grapefruit sections and chopped dill. Check the seasoning. Refrigerate until ready to use.

Halibut: Season the halibut cheeks on both sides with salt and pepper, and dredge one side with the yellow curry powder. In a large sauté pan over medium-high heat, add the remaining olive oil. When hot, lay the cheeks in curry side up. Saute until light brown, about 2 minutes. Turn over and sauté until a deep yellow-brown color is developed, about 4 minutes. Remove and set aside.

To Serve: Arrange the chilled beets in an overlapping spiral pattern on individual plates, being sure to alternate the golden and red beets. Season with salt and pepper. Ladle some of the emulsion on and around the beets. Make sure the grapefruit pieces are in some sort of pattern. Lay the halibut cheeks in a shingled pattern across the middle of the plate over the beets, at least 3 pieces per person. Garnish with dill sprigs.

Chilean Sea Bass en Papillote with Chanterelle Mushrooms, Fingerling Potatoes, White Asparagus & Bacon Butter

4 SERVINGS

Ingredients

Mustard Vinaigrette

1 small shallot, peeled

2 tablespoons Dijon mustard

1 teaspoon whole-grain mustard

¼ cup white wine vinegar

1 teaspoon chopped thyme leaves

½ teaspoon salt

1 teaspoon black pepper

1 ice cube

⅔ cup olive oil

Bacon Butter

¼ pound sliced bacon, cut in ¼-inch wide strips

¼ pound unsalted butter, room temperature

1 tablespoon finely minced shallot

En Papillote

4 sheets of parchment paper

1 pound fingerling potatoes, washed and cut in half, lengthwise

1 pound white asparagus, remove 1 inch off bottom

1 pound chanterelle mushrooms, end of stems trimmed, cleaned and torn in half

4 Chilean sea bass fillets (6 oz), skin off, bones removed

2 teaspoons kosher salt

½ teaspoon black pepper

¼ cup dry white wine

Method

Potatoes: Add the potatoes to a pot of salted cold water. Turn the heat to high and bring to a simmer. Reduce heat to medium and cook until just finished, about 20 minutes. Strain and cool completely.

While the potatoes are cooking, render the bacon. In a pan over medium heat, cook the bacon until crispy, about 10 to 12 minutes. Strain and save both the

bacon and cool the fat. Finely chop the bacon. Once the fat solidifies, combine the fat in a bowl with the butter, minced shallot and the bacon crumbles. Combine thoroughly and refrigerate.

Vinaigrette: In a blender, combine the shallot, mustards, white wine vinegar, thyme, salt, pepper, and the ice cube. With the blender running, add the oil in a slow steady stream. Check the seasoning and refrigerate.

En papillote: Preheat the oven to 450°F. Lay a piece of parchment paper facing lengthwise on a working surface. Just below the center of the paper, place ¼ of the potatoes. Next, arrange 4 stalks of asparagus across the potatoes and place a mound of chanterelles over and around the potatoes. Place 2 tablespoons of the bacon butter on top of the mushrooms. (Note: Make sure the filling is compact, because the paper will be folded over the fish and the edges crimped). Sprinkle ½ teaspoon of salt on the vegetables and place a piece of fish on top. Gently press down to settle the fish so it doesn't tip over during cooking. Sprinkle salt and pepper on the fish and splash 1 tablespoon of white wine over the fish. Fold the paper over and, starting at one edge, fold the paper over itself continuously to create crimped, closed edges. Continue all the way around. Repeat this process for the rest of the fish. Arrange the fish on a baking sheet without overcrowding them (use 2 baking sheets if necessary). Place the fish in the oven and cook for 15 minutes.

To Serve: Use a large spatula and transfer the fish to 4 dinner plates. Unwrap the edges and fold the paper back under itself, exposing the fish. Ladle some of the mustard sauce over and around the fish.

Note: "En papillote" or "in parchment" is one of the easiest, healthiest, and most versatile ways to prepare fish, particularly flaky white fish. The parchment retains all the juicy flavors tucked inside. There are endless combinations of fish, vegetables, sauces, and butters you can try, all nicely self-contained in a little package. We like to prepare this dish on busy nights in the restaurant because we can make them hours ahead and they are simple to plate. Serving them in paper and cutting it open at the table adds a real dramatic touch.

salt and pepper to season the outside of the 4 fish. Now lay 2 strips of bacon, touching side by side, on a cutting board. Square both ends off by cutting off about ¼ inch. The bacon strips should be long enough to overlap by about 1 inch once they're wrapped around the fish. Lay one trout across the center of the bacon and wrap with bacon. Transfer to a platter and repeat the process with the remaining fish.

In a large cast iron skillet or sauté pan over medium-high heat, add 2 table-spoons of the olive oil. Swirl the oil around to coat the pan, and, when hot, gently lay the trout down and sear (2 trout per pan if possible). Cook until the bacon begins to tighten and crisp, about 5 minutes. With a fish spatula, gently flip the fish over, add 1 tablespoon of butter and cook until the bacon crisps, about 3 minutes. Transfer the fish to an oiled baking sheet and repeat the process for the other fish. Place the baking sheet with the 4 fish in the oven for another 5 minutes.

While the fish is finishing, pour the excess oil out of the pan, turn the heat to high and add the wine. Using the back of a spatula, scrape up any of the flavorful bits and reduce the wine by half. Add the chopped thyme, a little salt and pepper and swirl in the remaining butter. Turn the heat off.

To Serve: Spoon an oblong-shaped portion of the lentils onto each of 4 dinner platters. Lay a trout on the lentils, and spoon some of the pan sauce on and around the fish.

Note: A side vegetable like the creamed corn (see page 289) makes a great accompaniment.

Miso Shrimp with Green Tea Rice, Marinated Mushrooms & Spicy Shiso Ponzu

6 SERVINGS

Ingredients

Shrimp

¼ cup sake

¼ cup mirin

¾ cup white miso paste

⅔ cup granulated sugar

¾ tablespoon sesame oil

1½ tablespoon grape seed oil

¼ cup water

36 large gulf shrimp, peeled and deveined with tail on

Ponzu Sauce MAKES 2 CUPS

¼ cup green hot sauce

1.4 cup soy sauce

¼ cup rice wine vinegar

¼ cup fresh lime juice

¼ cup grape seed oil

¼ cup red jalapeno (Fresno chili), finely diced

¼ cup white onion, peeled and small diced

2 tablespoons shiso leaf, finely chopped (available in Asian markets)

2 tablespoons fresh cilantro, finely chopped

Mushrooms

2 tablespoons unsalted butter

2 tablespoons olive oil

½ pound shiitake mushrooms, stems removed and sliced

½ pound button mushrooms, stems removed and sliced

½ pound oyster mushrooms, torn by hand into strips

1 tablespoon minced garlic

1 teaspoon red pepper flakes

1 bunch arugula, large stems removed, washed and spun dry

Mushroom Marinade

¼ cup soy sauce

2 tablespoons fresh lemon juice

2 tablespoons sesame oil

½ cup rice wine vinegar

2 tablespoons scallions, small diced

2 tablespoons ginger root, peeled and finely minced

2 tablespoons fresh cilantro, chopped

Rice

3 green tea bags

3½ cups water

3 cups Japanese sticky rice

¼ cup rice wine vinegar

¼ cup mirin

2 tablespoons kosher salt

2 teaspoons black sesame seeds

Method

Shrimp marinade: In a saucepan, over high heat, bring the sake and mirin to a boil for 2 minutes. Lower the heat to medium and slowly whisk in the miso paste, a little at a time, until a smooth consistency is achieved. Turn the heat back up to high and gradually whisk in the sugar, being careful not to burn. Remove from heat, let cool, then whisk in the sesame oil, grape seed oil and water. Cool completely, then toss the prawns in the marinade and refrigerate for 3 to 4 hours. This marinade can be made ahead of time.

Ponzu sauce: In a bowl, combine the hot sauce, soy sauce, rice wine vinegar, lime juice, grape seed oil, jalapeno, onion, shiso leaf and cilantro. Mix well and refrigerate until serving.

Marinated mushrooms: In a large sauté pan over high heat, add the butter and olive oil. When hot, add the mushrooms and sauté. Toss frequently, until the mushrooms lose all their moisture and begin to brown, about 12 to 15 minutes. Add the garlic and chili flakes. Toss the mushrooms a few more times, and let cool.

While the mushrooms are cooling, make the marinade by combining the soy sauce, lemon juice, sesame oil, rice wine vinegar, scallions, ginger root and cilantro. Mix well to combine, and pour over the cooled mushrooms. Toss with the arugula just before serving.

Rice: Begin by making tea using the tea bags and the water. Remove the bags and cool the tea.

Next, rinse the rice by adding rice to a large bowl with twice the amount of cold water. Swirl with hands and pour out the water. Repeat the process two or three times.

Add the rice, chilled tea, vinegar, mirin and salt in a rice cooker and cook according to manufacturer's directions. If a rice cooker is not on hand, place the ingredients into an uncovered pot, turn the heat on high and bring to a boil, stirring periodically. Immediately turn the heat to low, cover the rice and let cook until done, about 20 minutes. Turn the heat off, and let the rice sit for 5 minutes.

Shrimp: Soak 6 bamboo skewers in water. The shrimp are meant to be grilled, so turn on an outdoor grill or barbecue. Once the grill is hot, place the shrimp skewers on the grill and cook for about 3 minutes. Turn once and cook for an additional 3 minutes. (Note: Do not overcook the shrimp.)

To Serve: Give the ponzu sauce a stir and ladle a generous amount in the center of 6 dinner plates. Place a nice mound of the green tea rice in the center and sprinkle the black sesame seeds over the rice. Remove the shrimp from the skewers and arrange them, leaning the shrimp on the rice, in a circular pattern with the tails pointing upwards. Toss the arugula with the marinated mushrooms and place a generous amount on top.

Petrale Sole with Grilled Fennel & Orange-Pine Nut Brown Butter

4 SERVINGS

Ingredients

3 fennel bulbs, tops torn away from the large stems and reserved

3 tablespoons olive oil

2 tablespoons kosher salt

1 teaspoon black pepper

1 bunch arugula, washed, spun dry and large stems removed

2 oranges

1 cup all-purpose flour

1½ pound large petrale sole fillets

½ pound unsalted butter

¼ cup pine nuts, lightly toasted

2 tablespoons fresh lemon juice

1 tablespoon Italian flat leaf parsley, finely chopped

Method

HEAT AN OUTDOOR GRILL ON HIGH.

Slice two of the fennel bulbs in half and remove most of the core, leaving just enough so the wedges remain intact while cooking. Slice each half into 4 wedges. Next, finely chop 2 tablespoons of the fennel tops. Toss them in a bowl with the fennel wedges, 2 tablespoons olive oil, 1 teaspoon of salt and 1 pinch of black pepper. Lay the fennel wedges flat on the grill and cook one side for 4 minutes. Turn the wedges over and cook for another 4 minutes. Transfer the wedges to a parchment-lined baking sheet and reserve.

Slice the third fennel bulb in half and completely remove the core. Using a vegetable mandolin, and starting with the root end of the bulb, thinly slice the fennel into about ¹⁄₁₆-inch into a salad bowl. Slice only half of the fennel. Add the arugula to the bowl along with ¼ cup of the fennel fronds roughly torn by hand. Reserve.

Remove the ends from the orange and peel the outer rind down to the flesh. Section the oranges with a paring knife and reserve the sections. Squeeze the remaining juice from the innards and reserve.

Preheat the oven to 400°F.

Place the flour in a large container or plate, large enough to dredge the fish. Season the fish on one side with 1 tablespoon salt and remaining black pepper. Dredge both sides of the fish in the flour, shake off the excess, and lay on a plate. Place the baking sheet of fennel in the oven to warm.

In a sauté pan, large enough to hold two portions of fish, over high heat, add 2 tablespoons of butter. When the butter is hot, add the fish. Let brown slightly, about 2 minutes. Carefully flip the fillets over and cook for 2 additional minutes. Transfer the fish to a plate, wipe out the sauté pan and repeat the process with the remaining fish and 2 new tablespoons of butter.

When finished cooking the fish, turn the heat of the sauté pan to high, and add the remaining butter. When the butter is hot, add the toasted pine nuts, orange sections, 1 tablespoon of reserved orange juice, 1 tablespoon of lemon juice, remaining salt, and the chopped parsley. Cook for 20 seconds and remove from heat.

To Serve: On 4 dinner plates, arrange the grilled fennel in a shingled pattern across the center of the plate. Carefully lay equal amounts of fish on top of the fennel. Spoon some of the sauce on and around each fish, making sure to include the orange sections. Dress the shaved fennel salad with the remaining olive oil and lemon juice. Garnish with small tuft of the salad.

Note: Sometimes petrale sole comes in really small fillets, which is okay. Orange roughy also works great with this recipe as does halibut or sea bass. The brown butter sauce used here can be a little tricky the first time, but becomes second nature with practice. The trick is once the butter has foamed and begins to turn brown, add the citrus juice and quickly turn off the heat to avoid burning the butter.

Alaskan King Salmon with Chickpeas, Cumin, Olives & Rosemary

4 SERVINGS

Ingredients

2 cups dried chickpeas, soaked in 4 cups cold water overnight or canned

2 cups chicken stock

3 cups water

2 tablespoons kosher salt

4 salmon fillets (8 ounces each), skin on, scaled, pinbones removed

½ teaspoon black pepper

6 tablespoons olive oil

1 tablespoon minced garlic

2 tablespoons cumin seed, toasted and ground

1 teaspoon red pepper flakes

⅛ cup dry white wine

⅓ cup picholine olives, pitted and coarsely chopped

½ cup tomato juice

1 teaspoon anchovy paste

1 tablespoon finely chopped fresh rosemary

2 tablespoons unsalted butter

Method

Chickpeas: Once the peas have soaked overnight, drain and place in a pot. Cover with the chicken stock, water and 1 teaspoon of salt. Turn the heat to high, bring to a boil, reduce the heat to medium. Let simmer until the peas are tender, about 45 minutes. Drain the chickpeas, but reserve about 4 ounces of the cooking liquid.

Preheat the oven to 425°F.

With a sharp knife, score the skin side of the salmon to keep the skin from curling during cooking. (Note: Do this by applying a small amount of pressure as the knife is run across the width of the fish. Do not cut deep into the flesh. The score marks should be about 1 inch apart.) Season the salmon on both sides with salt and pepper. In a sauté pan, large enough to fit the 4 pieces of salmon, over high heat, add 3 tablespoons of olive oil. When hot, add the fish, flesh side down. Cook until a nice crust appears, about 3 minutes. Turn the fish over and continue to cook until the skin begins to crisp, about 3 minutes. Carefully transfer the fish to a baking sheet and place in the oven for 2 minutes.

While the fish is finishing in the oven, remove the excess oil from the sauté pan, place the pan back on the burner and add the remaining olive oil. Add the minced garlic, cumin and red pepper flakes. Saute for 10 seconds. Add the chickpeas, toss, and add the white wine. Reduce to almost dry and add the olives, tomato juice, reserved cooking liquid and anchovy paste. Stir to break up the anchovy paste. Cook for 3 minutes. Add the chopped rosemary and butter. Check the seasoning. There should be just enough of the sauce so it coats the chickpeas and slowly runs off.

To Serve: Arrange equal amounts of the chickpea mixture in the center of 4 dinner bowls. Place a piece of the salmon on top, and serve immediately.

Note: We love skin on the fish at the restaurant. When you can get the skin nice and crispy, it offers such a unique textural counterpoint. The sound of anchovy paste may deter some, but it melds so well with the tomato, olive and kick of the chili flake. You really don't know you are eating anchovy. This preparation will also work well with swordfish, snapper and tuna.

Crispy Garlic Chicken

4 SERVINGS

Ingredients

Marinade

1 cup canola oil

1 cup olive oil

1 cup garlic cloves peeled

2 tablespoons chopped parsley

1 teaspoon kosher salt

½ teaspoon black pepper

Chicken

2 whole chicken (½ chicken per serving)

2 tablespoons canola oil, for frying

1½ teaspoon kosher salt

¼ teaspoon black pepper

Method

To debone and prepare the Chicken: (please refer to the visual step-by-step process on pages 240 and 241). Beginning with the first chicken, remove the pair of wings and discard. With a finger, find the middle of the breast plate and insert knife alongside the breast bone. Slowly run the tip of the knife down the breast bone, and down the rib cage, separating the breast and leg meat from the carcass as if filleting a fish. The key is to keep the breast and leg meat together with the skin, while removing the complete side from the carcass. Repeat the process on the other side. Begin removing the leg-thigh bone from each side of meat. Use the tip of the knife and follow the leg-thigh bone while separating the bone from the meat. Once the bone is partially exposed, dislodge the bone by carefully cutting it away from the knuckle. Using both hands, grip the bone and pull away while sliding down the meat and skin with the other hand as if sliding down a sock. Discard the bone. The finished side will be the boneless breast and boneless leg meat held together by the outer skin. Repeat the process with the second chicken.

How to **Debone and Prepare** the Chicken

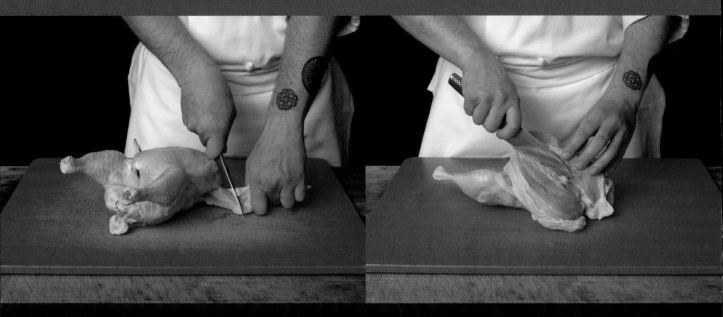

Step 1: Beginning with the first chicken, remove the pair of wings and discard.

Step 2: With a finger, find the middle of the breast plate and insert knife alongside the breast bone. Slowly run the tip of the knife down the breast bone and rib cage, separating the breast and leg meat from the carcass as if filleting a fish.

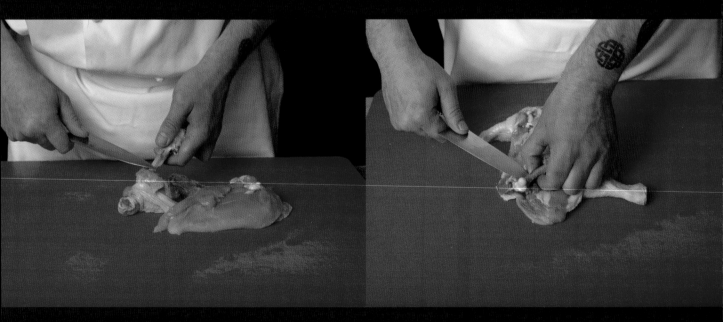

Step 5: Use the tip of the knife and follow the leg-thigh bone, while separating the bone from the meat.

Step 6: Once the bone is partially exposed, dislodge the bone by carefully cutting it away from the knuckle.

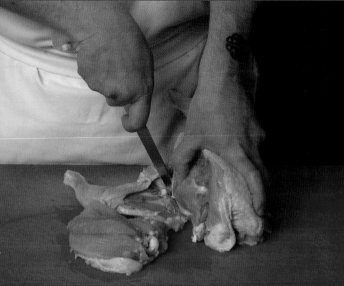

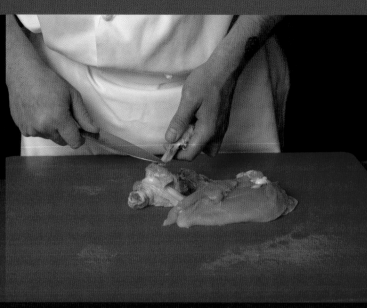

Step 3: The key is to keep the breast and leg meat together with the skin, while removing the complete side from the carcass. Repeat the process on the other side.

Step 4: Begin removing the leg-thigh bone from each side of meat.

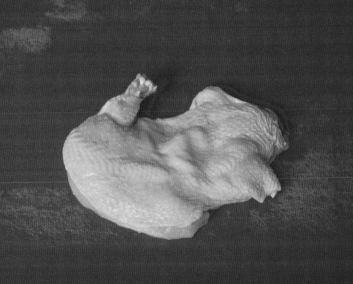

Step 7: Using both hands, grip the bone and pull away while sliding down the meat and skin with the other hand as if sliding down a sock. Discard the bone.

Step 8: The finished side will be the boneless breast and boneless leg meat held together by the outer skin. Repeat the process with the second chicken.

Marinade: In a heavy bottomed pot over medium heat, add the canola oil, olive oil and garlic cloves. Cook the garlic, stirring periodically, until the garlic is light brown, about 40 minutes. Remove from the heat and let steep for another 10 minutes. Remove the garlic and reserve. Cool the oil completely. Once the oil is cool, add the chopped parsley, salt and pepper. Pour the marinade over the chickens and let them marinate for at least 4 hours. (Note: reserve the cooked garlic for garnishing the chicken.)

To cook the chicken: Preheat the oven to 500°F. Remove the chicken from the marinade and season with salt and pepper. In two large ovenproof sauté pans over high heat, add the canola oil. When hot, add the chicken, 2 per pan, skin-side down. (Note: It is important that the chickens are not moved once they touch the pan.) Cook on high heat until crispy golden brown, about 4 minutes. Transfer the pans to the oven and cook for 6 minutes. Using a pair of tongs, turn the chicken over, now skin-side up. Continue to cook until the chicken is cooked through with an internal temperature of 165°F, about 10 minutes. Remove from oven.

In a separate sauté pan, over medium-high heat, add the roasted garlic and a little oil. Cook until garlic and oil are heated through. Remove from heat.

To Serve: Transfer the chicken to individual serving plates, ½ per serving. Pour the roasted garlic (about 6 or 7 cloves per serving) and pan oil over the chicken. Serve with a side of garlic mashed potatoes (see page 286).

Note: This is a preparation I learned while working at Spago and Campanile. The crispy garlic chicken has been our best-selling dish from day one. Many of our customers have never ordered anything else when dining at Bis.

including the top and bottom, about 10 minutes. Transfer the shanks to a roasting pan, and reserve at room temperature.

Discard the excess oil from the pan, and add 2 tablespoons of oil, diced carrot, onion, leek, celery and garlic cloves. Saute until light brown. Add the red wine and scrape the bottom of the pan. Stir well to incorporate, and pour the liquid contents into the roasting pan, along with the crushed tomatoes, sachet and warm stocks. Bring to a simmer and cover with foil. Braise in the oven for 2½ hours. Remove when the veal is about to fall off the bone. Strain and reserve the cooking liquid. Discard the vegetables.

Remove the veal from the braising liquid and remove the string. Reduce the braising liquid for 5 additional minutes. Season with 1 teaspoon of salt and ½ teaspoon of black pepper.

To Serve: Place one shank on each of 4 dinner plates. Spoon the sauce over each shank. In a bowl, mix the rosemary, pecans and orange zest. Sprinkle on top of each shank to garnish. Serve with plain rice, saffron risotto, mashed potatoes or even gnocchi.

Chipotle & Beer-Braised Beef Short Ribs with Green Chili & Goat Cheese Mashers

6 SERVINGS

Ingredients

Braised Beef

6 beef short ribs, English cut, 4 inches long with 2 inches of meat

2 tablespoons kosher salt

1 tablespoon black pepper

2¼ cups chicken stock

2¼ cups beef stock

2 bottles dark ale (Negro Modelo)

⅔ cup canned chipotle in adobo, pureed to a paste

3 cups canned diced tomato in juice

½ cup canola oil

2 carrots, peeled and roughly chopped

1 yellow onion, peeled and roughly chopped

2 stalks of celery, roughly chopped

2 jalapenos, stemmed and roughly chopped

1 tablespoon minced garlic

Sachet

Note: A sachet is a cheesecloth filled with herbs and spices and tied off with a piece of kitchen string.

1 bunch cilantro stems, tied with butcher's twine

2 teaspoons whole coriander

1 bay leaf

2 teaspoons black peppercorns

Potatoes

1 cup canned green chilies, drained and pureed

⅔ cup fresh-crumbled goat cheese

1 recipe garlic mashed potatoes (see page 286)

Method

PREHEAT THE OVEN TO 350°F.

Beef: Season the short ribs on all sides with salt and black pepper. In a large pot over high heat, add the chicken stock, beef stock, dark ale, pureed chipotles and the can of diced tomatoes with the juice. Bring to a simmer.

Meanwhile, in a large sauté pan over high heat, add 4 tablespoons of the canola oil. Bring to the smoking point and add 2 short ribs, meat-side down first. Sear until brown and repeat the process on all sides. Transfer the ribs to a large roasting or braising pan. Add more oil to the pan and repeat the process until all the ribs are seared. Next, add half of the chopped carrot, onion, celery, jalapeno, and garlic to the sauté pan. Saute until the vegetables are light brown. Add the sautéed vegetables to the roasting pan and repeat the process with the remaining vegetables. Add the sachet to the roasting pan and fill the pan with the hot cooking stock. The stock should cover the ribs about 1 inch. Cover the braising pan with two layers of foil and place on the center rack of the oven. Braise for 2½ to 3 hours (until the ribs are meltingly tender and almost falling off the bone).

Remove the short ribs from the braising liquid and set aside. Strain the liquid through a fine-mesh strainer into a sauce pot over high heat. Reduce the liquid for about 5 minutes.

Fold the pureed green chilies and goat cheese with the mashed potatoes, and stir until combined. The cheese does not have to melt all the way.

To Serve: Place a large scoop of the potatoes in the center of 4 dinner plates. Add one short rib to each plate and ladle some of the braising juices over the short rib. Serve the ribs with grilled zucchini or a side of creamed corn (see page 289).

Herb-Crusted Leg of Lamb with Oven-Dried Tomatoes & Truffled White Beans

8-10 SERVINGS

Ingredients

Lamb

1 leg of lamb, bone-in (approximately 10 to 12 pounds)

5 garlic cloves, peeled and split in half

2 tablespoons kosher salt

1½ tablespoon black pepper

1 tablespoon anchovy paste

1 tablespoon Dijon mustard

3 tablespoons olive oil

1 tablespoon fresh lemon juice

2 tablespoons chopped-fresh rosemary

2 tablespoons chopped-fresh Italian flat-leaf parsley

2 tablespoons chopped-fresh thyme

Beans

2 tablespoons olive oil

2 tablespoons unsalted butter

6 celery stalks, washed and small diced

1 carrot, peeled and small diced

1 yellow onion, peeled and small diced

1 leek (white part), small diced

½ fennel bulb, cored and small diced

1 cup dry white wine

4 tablespoons tomato paste

1 tablespoon kosher salt

1 tablespoon truffle salt (available at high-quality markets)

2 tablespoons chopped-fresh thyme

1 tablespoon black pepper

½ recipe oven dried tomatoes (see page 186), chopped

2 cups chicken stock

1 can (27 ounces) canned cannellini beans, rinsed

2 tablespoons white truffle oil

Method

Lamb: With a sharp pointed knife, make 10 slits all around the lamb. Push a piece of garlic in each slit. Season the entire leg with the salt and pepper. Let the leg sit at room temperature for 10 minutes.

While the lamb is tempering, in a small bowl combine the anchovy paste, mustard, 1 tablespoon of the olive oil and lemon juice. Mix together. In another small bowl, combine the chopped rosemary, parsley and thyme. Slather the wet mixture over the leg. Let sit for 30 minutes at room temperature.

Preheat the oven to 450°F.

Press the herb mixture over the lamb, making sure to evenly coat. Pour the remaining 2 tablespoons of olive oil in the bottom of a roasting pan. Set the leg of lamb in the roasting pan and place in the center rack of the oven. Cook for 10 minutes uncovered. Turn the oven down to 350°F. Turn the leg over and cook for 35 additional minutes. (Note: The internal temperature should reach 125 to 130°F; test with a thermometer at the thickest, deepest point.) Remove the leg from the oven, cover with foil, and let rest for 10 minutes at room temperature.

Beans: While the lamb is roasting, make the beans. In a large pan over high heat, add the olive oil and butter. Let the butter foam. Add the celery, carrot, onion, leek and fennel. Saute until tender, about 5 minutes. Add the white wine and reduce by half. Add the tomato paste, salt, truffle salt, chopped thyme, black pepper, chopped ovendried tomatoes, chicken stock and white beans. Reduce the heat to simmer and reduce to a sauce consistency. Finish with truffle oil and check the seasoning.

To Serve: This dish is meant to be served family style, but the initial presentation is the "wow" factor. Use a large serving platter and arrange the bean mixture in the center. Lay the entire leg of lamb on the beans. Present at the table with a carving knife. Serve with a side salad or steamed vegetables. The secret is to keep the presentation simple.

Maple-Brined Pork Loin Chop with Sweet Corn Fritters & Mustard Gratin

4 SERVINGS

Ingredients

Pork Chops

2 quarts water

⅓ cup kosher salt

½ cup maple syrup

⅓ cup bourbon

2 teaspoons ground mustard

1 bay leaf

½ teaspoon red chili flakes

2 teaspoons fresh rosemary, finely chopped

4 pork loin chops (12 ounces each)

Mustard Gratin

¼ pound sliced bacon, cut into ½-inch-wide pieces

½ yellow onion, peeled and small diced

1 teaspoon minced garlic

2 bunches mustard greens, stemmed and washed

1½ cups heavy cream

2 tablespoons Dijon mustard

Corn Fritters

2 quarts canola oil, for frying

Dry Ingredients

¾ cup yellow cornmeal

½ cup all-purpose flour

2 teaspoons baking powder

½ teaspoon granulated sugar

½ teaspoon kosher salt

Wet Ingredients

¾ cup buttermilk

1 whole egg

2 cups corn kernels

Method

Pork chops: In a sauce pot over medium-high heat, add the water, salt, maple syrup, bourbon, mustard, bay leaf, chili flakes and rosemary. Bring to a boil. Remove from heat and cool. Once the brine is cool, pat the pork chops dry with paper towels and place them in the brine. Make sure they are submerged. Refrigerate the chops for 24 hours. Remove from the brine, rinse under cold water and pat dry. Turn an outdoor grill on high. Place the pork chops on the grill and cook for 12 minutes, turning once. The chops should be medium to medium well.

Mustard gratin: Add the bacon to a large sauté pan and cook over medium-high heat until slightly crispy, about 8 minutes. Add the onion and garlic, and cook until the onions are translucent, about 3 minutes. Add the mustard greens and sauté for 2 minutes. Add the heavy cream and stir in the mustard. Turn to medium low and cook until cream thickens, about 4 minutes. Season with salt and pepper. Keep warm.

Fritters: In one mixing bowl combine the cornmeal, flour, baking powder, sugar and salt. Mix thoroughly. In another bowl, combine the buttermilk and egg. Beat together and fold the wet ingredients into the dry ingredients until just combined. Fold in the corn kernels just before frying. To fry, add the oil in a heavy-bottomed pot over medium-high heat. Use a candy thermometer to get the oil to 350°F. With 2 large spoons, create football shapes using the fritter batter. Carefully submerge them into the frying oil. Cook the fritters until they are golden brown. Remove each fritter as they're finished and drain on paper towels.

To Serve: Place a spoonful of the mustard-bacon sauce in the center of each of 4 dinner plates. Place a pork chop on top and 3 fritters around the chop.

Note: Brining is a smart way to ensure moistness in cuts of meat or poultry that can sometimes dry out. In this case, the maple in the brine creates depth of flavor and also builds a nice caramelization on the grilled chop.

Spicy Thin
Pork Chops

SERVES 4

Ingredients

4 ounces olive oil

1½ teaspoon dried oregano

1½ tablespoons fresh chopped oregano

¼ teaspoon garlic powder

½ teaspoon onion powder

1½ teaspoon kosher salt

¼ teaspoon fresh-cracked black pepper

½ teaspoon cayenne pepper

3 medium garlic cloves, peeled and crushed

2½ pounds thin pork loin chops, bone-in

Fresh lemon wedges, for garnish

Method

In a medium-size bowl, mix the olive oil with the dried oregano, fresh oregano, garlic powder, onion powder, salt, pepper and cayenne. Crush the garlic cloves in a press and add to the mixture. Add the pork chops, mix together, and marinate for a minimum of 2 hours.

Sear the pork chops over medium-high to high heat, depending on thickness, about 1½ to 3 minutes per side, or until slightly pink near the bone (be careful not to overcook). Remove from heat and serve with a wedge of fresh lemon.

Note: These chops pair well with panfried potatoes or spaghetti marinara.

Spice-Rubbed Duck Breast with Acorn Squash Hash and Sweet & Sour Cherries

4 SERVINGS

Ingredients

½ recipe duck confit rub (see pages 234-235)

4 large duck breasts

¼ pound sliced bacon, cut into ½-inch-wide pieces

2 tablespoons unsalted butter

1 tablespoon minced garlic

¼ pound cippolini onions, peeled and cut into quarters

1 acorn squash, seeded, peeled and cut into 1-inch pieces

1 carrot, peeled and cut into 1-inch pieces

1 Yukon gold potato, cut into 1-inch pieces

1 tablespoon fresh sage, chopped

1 teaspoon Italian flat-leaf parsley, chopped

2 tablespoons kosher salt

1½ teaspoon black pepper

1 teaspoon olive oil

¼ pound pitted bing cherries

¼ pound dried bing cherries, cut in half

½ recipe rich poultry jus (see page 143)

Method

Use 1 teaspoon of the spice rub, and thoroughly rub the skin side of the duck breast. Set aside.

In a large sauté pan, over medium-high heat, add the bacon. Stir frequently and cook until the bacon is close to crispy. Remove the bacon and reserve. Add 1 tablespoon of butter to the bacon fat, and melt. Add the garlic and cippolini onions, and cook until translucent, about 7 minutes. Add the acorn squash, carrots and potatoes. Stir frequently and cook until the edges of the squash and potatoes start to soften, about 10 to 12 minutes. Add the sage, parsley, bacon pieces, 1½ teaspoons of salt and ½ teaspoon black pepper. Stir to incorporate. Turn off the heat, and keep warm.

While the hash is finishing, add the oil in a large sauté pan over medium-high heat. Score the duck breasts on the skin side using a sharp knife and making slight cuts on the bias. This will allow the duck to render evenly and not curl up as the skin tightens. Season the duck breasts on both sides with salt and pepper. Lay them skin-side down in the oil and begin rendering. Cook until the skin is golden crispy brown, about 5 to 7 minutes. If the edges start to burn before the skin is browned, reduce the heat to medium. Turn the duck over and cook for 4 more minutes until the breast is medium rare. Remove from pan and let rest.

Remove all but 1 tablespoon of the fat in the pan and add the cherries. Saute for 20 seconds and add the rich poultry jus. Reduce by ⅓. Swirl in the butter and season with salt and pepper.

To Serve: Arrange a bed of hash in the center of 4 dinner plates. Place the duck breasts on a cutting board flesh-side up. With a sharp knife, firmly slice the duck into ¼-inch slices on the bias, through the skin. Flip the duck over and fan the duck slices over the top of the hash. Spoon some of the sauce on and around the duck and serve.

Note: Basically any green vegetable would make a great accompaniment with this dish. Sauteed greens work well too. Peeling the acorn squash can be tricky for some people because of its ridged texture. Butternut squash is a fine substitute for this.

Grilled Beef Tenderloin with Radicchio, Charred Tomatoes & Italian Salsa Verde

4 SERVINGS

Ingredients

Salsa Verde

2 bunches fresh Italian flat-leaf parsley, washed, stemmed and roughly chopped

2 tablespoons shallots, minced

3 garlic cloves, peeled

½ cup capers

½ cup cornichons (baby pickles)

2 anchovy fillets

2 tablespoons white wine vinegar

2 tablespoons lemon juice

1½ cups extra virgin olive oil

1 tablespoon Dijon mustard

1 teaspoon Kosher salt

½ teaspoon black pepper

Beef

1 whole beef tenderloin, fat and silver skin removed

2 tablespoons olive oil

3 tablespoons kosher salt

½ teaspoon black pepper

1 pound asparagus, bottom 2 inches removed

2 heads radicchio, halved and cut into wedges

4 Roma tomatoes, halved lengthwise

Method

Salsa verde: Combine the parsley, shallots, garlic, capers, cornichons and anchovies in a food processor. Pulse 4 or 5 times. Add the white wine vinegar, lemon juice, olive oil, mustard, salt and pepper, and pulse 8 more times. Set aside.

Turn on an outdoor grill to high heat. Brush the tenderloin with olive oil and season generously with salt and pepper. Place on the grill and deeply char all sides, about 20 minutes. (Note: Closing the lid periodically enhances the flavor.) Remove the tenderloin when the internal temperature of the thickest part reaches 130°F. Allow the beef to rest for 8 to 10 minutes before slicing and serving.

Toss the asparagus, radicchio and tomatoes separately with olive oil, salt and pepper. Arrange the vegetables on the grill and cook to desired doneness. Make sure the tomatoes get a nice char, but don't completely fall apart.

To Serve: This dish is meant to be presented family style, so begin by slicing the beef on the bias, about ½ inch thick. Place the beef in the center of a large serving platter, giving the meat a shingled appearance. Arrange the vegetables in a nice pattern around the tenderloin and ladle some sauce right over the beef, reserving some of the sauce to serve on the side.

Veal Rib Chop with Porcini, Rosemary & Swiss Chard

4 SERVINGS

Ingredients

Veal

4 single-bone veal rib chops
(12 to 14 ounces each)

1½ tablespoon kosher salt

1 teaspoon black pepper

2 tablespoons olive oil

1 pound porcini mushrooms, cut
into wedges, stem on

2 shallots, peeled and thinly sliced into rounds

1 teaspoon minced garlic

¼ cup dry white wine

¼ cup chicken stock

2 tablespoons crushed tomatoes

2 tablespoons heavy cream

1½ tablespoon fresh rosemary, finely minced

Swiss Chard

2 tablespoons olive oil

2 bunches Swiss chard, torn away from
the ribs, washed and dried

1 tablespoon lemon juice

1 teaspoon salt

½ teaspoon black pepper

Method

PREHEAT THE OVEN TO 425°F.

Veal: Season the veal chops with salt and pepper on both sides. In a large sauté pan with an ovenproof handle, over medium-high heat, add the olive oil. When hot, add the veal chops. Cook until the chops are brown on one side, about 5 minutes. Turn over and lay the mushrooms in the pan so they touch the bottom. Stir the mushrooms for 1 minute and place pan in the oven. Cook until the chops have an internal temperature of 135°F, about 7 to 9 minutes. Remove the pan and let the chops rest.

Place the pan with the mushrooms over medium heat. Add the shallots and garlic, and sauté for 1 minute. Add the white wine and chicken stock. Reduce by ⅓, about 2 minutes. Add the tomatoes, salt, pepper, cream and rosemary. Cook for 2 minutes. Remove from heat and reserve.

Chard: In another large sauté pan, over high heat, add the oil. When hot, add the chard and sauté, stirring and tossing frequently until the chard breaks down, about 2 minutes. Add the lemon juice, salt and pepper. Transfer the chard to paper towels to drain.

To Serve: Arrange the Swiss chard in the center of 4 dinner plates. Place a veal chop on top of the chard and spoon the mushroom sauce over and around the chop.

Customers always comment on what a great staff we have, and it's true. Our employees stick with Bis for far longer than the industry standard. I know it is tied to more than just my handsome charm.

Polenta-Stuffed Oregon Quail with Blackberries & Hazelnuts

4 SERVINGS (OR 8 AS AN APPETIZER)

Ingredients

Quail

8 semi-boneless quail

1 tablespoon kosher salt

1 teaspoon black pepper

½ recipe creamy polenta, cooled (see page 290, first step)

4 tablespoons olive oil

2 tablespoons unsalted butter

1 tablespoon minced shallots

1½ cups fresh blackberries, half pureed in a blender

½ recipe rich poultry jus (see page 143)

⅓ cups hazelnuts, toasted and roughly chopped

1 teaspoon fresh thyme, chopped

2 heads frisee lettuce, washed

Method

PREHEAT THE OVEN TO 425°F.

Tear 8 pieces of aluminum foil, about 5 inches long. Fold each piece about ¾ inch in width, and keep folding it over itself until a ¾-inch band of thick foil is achieved. These will be used to hold the quail in position and keep the polenta from leaking out. Repeat the process for the remaining foil. Set aside.

Season each quail with salt and pepper. Hold the cavity open and fill the quail with the cooled polenta until almost full, about 3 tablespoons. Spray the foil strips with some nonstick spray. Wrap a piece of foil around the quail so the end to be twisted close is situated where the cavity opening is. Make sure the wings are outside the foil, and the legs are above the foil and slightly crossed. Twist the foil firmly so it cinches against the cavity opening.

Place a large sauté pan over medium-high heat. (Note: This may require two pans.) Add the oil in the pan. When hot, begin searing the quail. Lay them on their sides first and sear until a nice brown color starts to appear, about 3 minutes. Repeat on the edges, top, and bottom. This will take about 8 minutes. Once the quail are seared, transfer the quail to a parchment-lined baking sheet and place them in the oven to finish cooking. Reserve the sauté pan. Roast the quail for about 10 minutes, or until the center of the polenta is hot.

While the quail are cooking, remove the excess oil from the sauté pan. Turn the heat to high, add 1 tablespoon of butter and quickly sauté the shallots, about 10 seconds. Add the whole blackberries, and sauté for 10 more seconds. Add the rich poultry jus, and reduce by ¼. Add the pureed blackberries, hazelnuts and thyme. Swirl in the remaining butter and season with salt and pepper.

To Serve: Place a small mound of frisee lettuce in the center of 4 dinner plates. Remove the quail from the oven and carefully untwist and remove the foil. (Caution: Foil will be hot.) Firmly cut the quail in half through the breast. Lay 4 halves of quail on each plate in a shingled pattern. Alternate polenta faceup and facedown on each plate. Ladle the sauce over the quail. Finish with hazelnuts and blackberries on each plate.

Side Dishes

Roasted Brussels Sprouts with Pancetta, Walnuts & Honey

4 TO 6 SERVINGS

Ingredients

1 teaspoon canola oil

½ pound pancetta, cut into ½-inch pieces

2 pounds Brussels sprouts, brown end trimmed off and halved

1 cup walnut pieces

4 tablespoons unsalted butter

1 tablespoon kosher salt

1 teaspoon black pepper

1 teaspoon fresh rosemary, finely chopped

2 tablespoons clover honey

Method

PREHEAT THE OVEN TO 350°F.

In a sauté pan over medium heat, add the canola oil and pancetta, stirring occasionally. Render the pancetta until almost crispy, about 15 minutes. Drain and reserve the pancetta fat. (Note: This step can be done in advance.)

While the pancetta is rendering, bring a large pot of generously salted water to a boil. Set up a bowl of ice water alongside (this will be used to "shock" the Brussels and stop them from cooking further). Add the Brussels sprouts to the boiling water and allow to cook for about 3 minutes (the exposed inner part of the stem should just start to look translucent). Remove from the water and plunge immediately into the ice water. When cool, remove the Brussels sprouts from the water and drain thoroughly on paper towels. (Note: This step can also be done in advance).

Arrange the walnut pieces on a baking sheet, and place them in the oven. Allow to lightly toast, about 5 minutes. (Note: Do not overtoast the nuts or they will become bitter; this step can also be done in advance.)

In a large sauté pan over high heat, add the butter and reserved pancetta fat. Cook until the butter begins to brown. Add the Brussels and continue to cook, stirring occasionally, until the Brussels sprouts are thoroughly brown, about 8 to 10 minutes. (Note: It's okay for some of the leaves to fall off and even become burned looking.) Add the salt, pepper and pancetta pieces. Cook for another minute, tossing frequently. Add the rosemary, walnuts and honey. Toss for another 30 seconds. Do not cook the honey too long. The sprouts should look deep brown and slightly glossy.

To Serve: Transfer to a serving platter, arrange, and serve immediately.

Note: Thoroughly draining and allowing the Brussels sprouts to dry is a crucial step. If there is excess water, the Brussels will steam and not sauté properly. It is important that the Brussels sprouts develop a crusty, caramelized look.

It is my job to make certain the staff has a great work environment. They need to make a good living, they need to know they are appreciated, and they have to feel confident about what we serve and how we go about serving it.

Morel Mushrooms with Fava Beans & Lavender

SERVINGS

Ingredients

2 pounds fresh fava beans

1 tablespoon olive oil

3 tablespoons unsalted butter

1 teaspoon minced garlic

1 tablespoon minced shallot

2 pounds morel mushrooms, halved lengthwise and thoroughly cleaned

½ teaspoon dried lavender, finely ground in a spice or coffee grinder

1 tablespoon fresh tarragon, chopped

½ tablespoon kosher salt

½ teaspoon black pepper

Method

Fava beans: Bring a small, generously salted pot of water to a boil. Also set up a small bowl of ice water to cool the fava beans. Next, split the bean pods open lengthwise and drop the favas in the boiling water, discarding the pods. As soon as the beans float to the surface, they are done. Quickly scoop the beans out and plunge them into the ice water. The beans will cool quickly. Next, scrape a small hole on each bean and gently squeeze the bean from its outer shell. (Note: The favas should be vibrant green; discard drab yellowish ones.) This step can be done in advance.

In a large sauté pan over medium-high heat, add the oil and butter. Allow to foam, and add the garlic, shallots and morel mushrooms. Shake the pan frequently to combine ingredients, and continue to cook until all the water has evaporated from the mushrooms, about 10 to 12 minutes. Add the dried lavender, tarragon, salt, pepper and the cooked fava beans. Toss a couple more times and remove from heat.

To Serve: Transfer to a serving platter, arrange, and serve immediately.

Note: Morel mushrooms are one of the true gems of the spring season. However, because they are often found near beaches, sand can be found lurking in every crevice of the mushrooms. Even the highest-quality morels need to be thoroughly cleaned, because the crunch of sand between your teeth will make you quickly forget what a treasure morels are. Our local forager tells us to submerge them in 3 or 4 changes of room temperature water. Gently agitate them with your hands to loosen the sand. Allow the sand to settle, then repeat the process 2 or 3 times. Drain the morels and allow them to dry for a bit on paper towels. We like to cut them in half lengthwise before adding them to the water, to expedite the cooking process. Fiddlehead ferns are also a great compliment to this dish when in season. Blanche the ferns in salted water and add to the dish with the fava beans.

Cumin-Scented Baby Carrots

4 TO 6 SERVINGS

Ingredients

3 bunches baby carrots or thumbelina carrots

2 tablespoons olive oil

1½ tablespoon ground cumin

2 teaspoons kosher salt

1 teaspoon black pepper

Zest of 1 orange

2 tablespoons unsalted butter

Method

PREHEAT THE OVEN TO 425°F.

Cut the tops off the baby carrots, leaving 1 inch of the green attached to the carrot. Rinse the carrots, but do not peel them. (Note: If some of the carrots seem too thick to roast, cut them in half lengthwise). Using a potato scrubber or a clean, mildly coarse scrub pad and brush, scrub the carrots in a downward motion to remove any excess dirt and particles.

Toss the carrots in a bowl with the olive oil, ground cumin, salt and pepper. Use a microplane to finely zest the orange into the carrots. Mix thoroughly, and lay in a single layer on a parchment-lined sheet pan. Place in the oven and roast until just done, about 15 minutes. Just before the carrots are finished, place a large sauté pan over medium heat. Melt the butter and transfer the carrots to the pan. Toss a few times and serve family style.

Note: We don't peel baby carrots when they are available because, like many of the sweet root vegetables, most of their sugars are just beneath the skin.

Garlic Mashed Potatoes

Ingredients

1¼ pound Yukon gold potatoes, peeled and cut into 1-inch chunks

1¼ pound russet potatoes, peeled and cut into 1-inch chunks

8 garlic cloves, peeled and split

¼ cup heavy cream

½ pound unsalted butter, room temperature, cut into cubes

3 teaspoons kosher salt

1 teaspoon white pepper

Method

Add the Yukon and russet potatoes along with the garlic cloves to a pot of cold water with 1 teaspoon salt. Bring to a simmer over medium heat and continue to cook until fork tender, about 15 minutes. In a sauce pot over low heat, add the heavy cream, just to warm. Drain the potatoes thoroughly, about 5 minutes. Transfer to a fitted bowl of a standing mixer, and add the butter. Using the paddle attachment, turn the mixer on medium speed. Add the salt and white pepper, and mix until the potatoes are emulsified with the butter, about 1 minute. Remove the bowl and fold in the warm cream. Keep warm until ready to serve.

Creamed Spinach

Ingredients

2 pounds fresh spinach, large stems removed

2 tablespoons unsalted butter

1 leek (white part), rinsed and medium diced

1 tablespoon minced garlic

1 cup heavy cream

¼ teaspoon grated nutmeg

2 teaspoons kosher salt

½ teaspoon black pepper

¼ cup grated Parmesan cheese

Method

PREHEAT THE OVEN TO 450°F.

Bring a large pot of salted water to a boil. When boiling, add the spinach and cook for 2 minutes. Remove the spinach from the water and plunge into a bowl of ice water. When cool, remove the spinach, and drain well, squeezing out as much liquid out as possible. Roughly chop the spinach, and set aside. In a large bowl, over high heat, melt the butter. Add the leeks and garlic, and sauté until the leeks are translucent, about 2 minutes. Add the chopped spinach, toss a few times, and add the cream, nutmeg, salt and pepper. Reduce the heat to medium and simmer until the liquid thickens slightly, about 7 minutes. Transfer the spinach to a baking dish, top with Parmesan and finish in the oven for 5 additional minutes. Remove from the oven and serve.

Braised Red Cabbage with Chestnuts & Apples

6 SERVINGS

Ingredients

2 tablespoons olive oil

2 tablespoons unsalted butter

1 small yellow onion, peeled, and ½-inch julienne (thinly sliced)

1 head of red cabbage, quartered, cored and julienned

1 apple, peeled, cored, and ½-inch dice

2 cups red wine

1 cup balsamic vinegar

2 tablespoons brown sugar

2 tablespoons kosher salt

1 teaspoon black pepper

1½ tablespoon chopped-fresh thyme

½ cup roasted chestnuts, chopped (available frozen or in gourmet cheese departments)

Method

In a large high-sided pan, over high heat, add the olive oil and butter. Once the butter is hot, add the onions, and sauté for 5 minutes. Add the cabbage and apples, and sauté until the cabbage has softened and shrunken down, about 8 to 10 minutes. Add the red wine, balsamic vinegar, brown sugar, salt and pepper. Cook uncovered until soft, about 15 minutes. Add the chopped thyme and chestnuts. Stir to incorporate. Remove and cool.

Note: This is a great fall and winter vegetable. Cabbage is versatile, and can go with fish or meat. We like to add it with salmon or pork chops. Chestnuts can sometimes be difficult to find, but the nuts you'll find in the grocery store will already be peeled, so all you have to do is thaw, toss with a little oil, and roast the nuts for 10 minutes before cooling and chopping.

Creamed Corn with Tarragon

4 TO 6 SERVINGS

Ingredients

2 tablespoons unsalted butter

1 yellow onion, peeled, small diced

1 teaspoon minced garlic

8 ears yellow corn, shucked, rinsed, kernels removed, milk scraped out and reserved

1 cup heavy cream

2 tablespoons buttermilk

2 tablespoons fresh tarragon leaves, chopped and stems reserved

2 teaspoons kosher salt

½ teaspoon black pepper

Method

In a large sauté pan, over medium heat, melt the butter. Add the onion and garlic, and sweat until translucent. Add the corn kernels and reserved corn milk. Saute until the mixture begins to dry out, about 5 minutes. Add the heavy cream, buttermilk, and the tarragon leaves and stems. Cook until the mixture thickens slightly, remove the tarragon stems, and add the salt, pepper and chopped tarragon. Remove from heat and serve family style.

Crispy Polenta Cakes

6 SERVINGS

Ingredients

7 cups hot water

2½ tablespoons kosher salt

1¾ cup polenta

1 teaspoon fresh rosemary, finely chopped

1 teaspoon black pepper

⅛ cup finely grated Parmesan

2 quarts vegetable oil, for frying

Kosher salt, as needed

Method

In a sauce pot, over high heat, add the water and salt. Cover and bring to a boil. Add the polenta, whisking constantly for 5 minutes, being sure to scrape the bottom and sides of the pot. As the polenta thickens, reduce the heat to medium, whisking less frequently. Add the rosemary and black pepper. Cook for 8 to 10 minutes, or until the polenta is of porridge consistency. Add the Parmesan and check the seasoning. Remove from the heat and spread the polenta (about ½ inch thick) onto a baking sheet (approximately 6 by 8 inches) sprayed with nonstick spray. Cool in the refrigerator for at least 3 hours.

In a heavy-bottomed pot, cast iron skillet, or countertop fryer, bring the oil to 350°F (use a candy thermometer). When the polenta is cooled, turn the polenta pan upside down over a cutting board. Cut the polenta cakes into desired shape or size (including a French-fry shape).

Ease the polenta pieces into the fryer oil in a single layer. (Note: The polenta will sink, but do not touch them. They need to set.) After 2 minutes of frying, gently ease them up from the bottom of the pan with a metal spatula. Let fry for another 3 to 4 minutes, or until they are deep golden-yellow and crispy. Remove the polenta from the oil and transfer to paper towels. Sprinkle with salt and arrange on a platter.

Duck Fat &
Rosemary Fingerling
Potatoes

4 TO 6 SERVINGS

Ingredients

2 quarts duck fat, melted (available at gourmet grocers and some meat departments)

2½ pound fingerling potatoes, rinsed and cut in half lengthwise

3 tablespoons unsalted butter

2 teaspoons minced garlic

2 tablespoons fresh rosemary, chopped

1½ tablespoon kosher salt

1½ teaspoon black pepper

Method

In a large pot, over medium-high heat, add the melted duck fat and fingerling potatoes. Let simmer, stirring periodically so the potatoes don't stick to the bottom. Reduce heat to medium and continue to cook until the potatoes are just tender, about 20 minutes.

Drain the potatoes and cool (the fat can be frozen for use later). Heat the butter in a large sauté pan over medium-high heat. Add the garlic and let sweat, about 2 minutes. Add the potatoes, rosemary, salt and pepper. Toss a few times to mix and serve family style.

Note: The flavor of these potatoes is reliant on the duck fat. Besides its many uses, duck fat stores well—both refrigerated and frozen for long periods of time. The fat can also be reused numerous times, so long as you don't burn it. Duck fat may seem like an odd ingredient to have on hand, but it pays for itself over and over again.

Desserts

Vanilla Crème Brulee

Ingredients

1¼ cup + 6 teaspoons granulated sugar

2 vanilla beans, split lengthwise

1 quart heavy cream

12 egg yolks

Method

PREHEAT THE OVEN TO 300°F.

In a pot, steep the 1¼ cup sugar, vanilla beans and cream over low heat for 30 minutes, stirring occasionally.

Transfer the mixture to a bowl and cool in an ice bath, stirring constantly until the cream mixture is below 40°F. Add the egg yolks and stir to incorporate them evenly into the cream mixture. Strain through a fine sieve to remove any lumps of egg and vanilla beans.

Place 6 creme brulee ramekins in a baking dish that allows space between them. Divide the mixture evenly among the ramekins. Carefully pour cold water in the baking dish until it is halfway up the sides of the ramekins. Be sure not to let any water get inside the ramekins.

Carefully place dish in the preheated oven. Cook uncovered until custard is set, approximately 1 hour. Do not let custards brown. When set, carefully remove ramekins from the water bath and place them in the refrigerator to cool and set completely, approximately 3 to 4 hours.

To Serve: Top the custards with the remaining sugar (1 teaspoon per rame-kin), tilting and turning the ramekins for even coating. Turn on a kitchen torch and hold the flame about 1 inch from the top of the brulees. Caramelize the sugar by moving the torch constantly for even coloring. Serve immediately.

Fortunately, I resisted the urge to have servers on roller skates singing opera. I just stuck to the basics. This turned out to be a good choice for me.

Molten Chocolate Cake

6 SERVINGS

Ingredients

6 ounces unsalted butter

6 ounces semisweet chocolate chips

3 egg yolks

3 whole eggs

3 ounces granulated sugar

⅛ teaspoon salt

¾ teaspoons all-purpose flour

¼ teaspoon vanilla extract

Chocolate shavings, for garnish

Vanilla ice cream

Method

In a double boiler, melt the butter. Once melted, add the chocolate chips and stir until a smooth homogenous mixture is achieved.

In a fitted bowl of a standing mixer (or use a hand mixer), place the egg yolks, whole eggs, sugar, salt, flour and vanilla extract. With the whisk attachment, mix on high until the egg mixture thickens and ribbons form. Turn the mixer down to medium and slowly add the chocolate mixture into the egg mixture.

Spray the inside of 6 dessert ramekins (5 to 6 oz) with nonstick baking spray. This will help the cake to rise evenly. Using a rubber spatula, scrape the insides of the mixing bowl to completely incorporate the chocolate-egg mixture. Fill each ramekin ¾ full. Place the ramekins in refrigerator to cool completely, about 2 hours.

Preheat the oven to 400°F. Place the ramekins on a baking sheet and bake for approximately 20 minutes. The cakes will rise and should have a very slight jiggle in the center.

To Serve: Serve the cakes hot, topped with chocolate shavings or a scoop of vanilla ice cream.

Note: This is one of the easiest desserts to make, and has become a legend at Bis on Main. There would be anarchy if we ever tried to take it off the menu!

I invite you to experience Bis on Main. For those who already have, I welcome you back.

Pecan Pie

Ingredients

Dough

2¼ cups all-purpose flour, sifted

¼ cup powdered sugar, sifted

⅛ teaspoon kosher salt

10 ounces unsalted butter, chilled, cut into small cubes

2 tablespoons cold water

Pie Filling

8 whole eggs

½ cup dark corn syrup

½ cup granulated sugar

1 cup brown sugar

1 teaspoon vanilla extract

⅛ teaspoon kosher salt

6 cups pecan halves

Method

Dough: Add half the flour, and all the sugar and salt to a fitted bowl of a standing mixer (or use a hand mixer). Using the paddle attachment, turn the mixer on low. While it's running, add the butter a few chunks at a time until it is all used. Add the remaining flour and cold water. Turn the mixer to medium and run until there are no visible chunks of butter and the dough is smooth, not tacky to the touch.

Press the dough into an 8-inch round, wrap with plastic and refrigerate for 1 hour.

Preheat the oven to 300°F.

Remove the dough from the refrigerator and allow to reach room temperature and slightly stiff, about 20 minutes.

I want Bis on Main to be an extension of my home.
I want it to be my *Cheers*.

Lightly flour a work surface and spread some flour on all sides of the dough as well. Press the dough to make a slightly larger round. Rub some flour on a rolling pin and roll the dough out to about ⅛ inch thick and 14 inches in diameter. Lightly brush oil in a 9-inch by 2-inch-deep removable bottom pie tin. Roll the dough onto the rolling pin and transfer to the pie tin. Beginning at the nearest edge of the tin, leave about ½ inch of dough hanging over the edge, and gently let the dough drop over the tin. Tuck the dough down into the corners, being careful not to tear the dough. Once the dough is tucked down into the crevices and along the edges, gently scrape away the excess dough so the top of the shell is even with the top of the tin. Use any of the scraps to patch holes and discard the rest.

Filling: In a mixing bowl, beat the eggs. Add the corn syrup, granulated sugar, brown sugar, vanilla and salt. Whisk until the ingredients are combined and smooth (the brown sugar will clump at first). Place the pie tin on a baking sheet. Fill the shell evenly with the pecans. Pour the pie filling over the pecans until the filling comes to just below the top of the crust and the pecans are covered.

Place the baking sheet in the center rack of the oven and bake for 2 hours. After 2 hours, the pecans should have risen and the filling should have a puffed-up look. Press gently. If the center is still liquid, continue cooking—checking every 10 minutes until set. Remove the pie and let cool completely at room temperature, at least 2 or 3 hours. (Note: If not serving the pie at this point, place the pie in the refrigerator to cool completely.)

To Serve: If you are serving the pie from room temperature "cooled," then hold the edge of the pie tin firmly with one hand, and with the other hand gently push up on the removable bottom. Once you have created a small opening, run your fingers along the inside ledge of the tin until it is completely loose. Remove the bottom. Set the pie on a cutting board and, using a serrated bread knife, gently cut through the crust, which will be fairly thick. Place in a 350°F oven for about 5 minutes to warm. Top with whip cream or vanilla ice cream and serve. Note: If you choose to refrigerate the pie and serve later, follow the same process (except for the heating process). Cut the pie as described, but once cut, heat each piece in a microwave for about 1 minute, just to remove the chill.

Pear & Almond Tart with Brandied Caramel

6 SERVINGS

Ingredients

Pears

1 bottle semidry riesling

1 cinnamon stick

2 whole cloves

⅛ teaspoon ground nutmeg

¼ teaspoon ground allspice

2 star anise

3 bosc or bartlett pears

6 scoops of vanilla ice cream

Tart Batter

1¼ cup Marcona almonds or sliced almonds

½ cup granulated sugar

⅓ cup all-purpose flour

⅛ teaspoon kosher salt

2 eggs

¼ cup whole milk

4 tablespoons melted butter

3 teaspoons butter, cut into 6 pieces, room temperature

Brandied Caramel MAKES ABOUT ¾ CUP

½ cup granulated sugar

2 tablespoons water

⅛ teaspoon fresh lemon juice

1 tablespoon brandy

3 ounces heavy cream

Method

Pears: In a pot over medium heat, combine the riesling, cinnamon, whole cloves, nutmeg, allspice and star anise. Whisk until the sugar is dissolved. Next, peel and core the pears. Add the pears to the liquid. Cut a piece of wax or parchment paper so it fits inside the pot and cover the pears with

the paper, sealing along the edges. Poke a small hole in the center of the paper to allow steam to escape. Let the pears cook until they are soft with a touch of firmness when squeezed, about 30 minutes. With a slotted spoon, remove the pears, slice them in half lengthwise, place in an uncovered container and cool them in the refrigerator. Strain and cool the liquid. (Note: The pears can be stored in the liquid if you are making them ahead, otherwise discard the liquid.)

Tart batter: Preheat the oven to 350°F. In a food processor, combine the almonds, sugar, flour and salt. Grind until the mixture is dry and slightly crumbly. With the processor still running, add the eggs and milk. Once they are incorporated, add in the melted butter and mix until incorporated.

Place six 4-inch removable-bottom tart pans on a baking sheet and spray the inside with nonstick baking spray or butter. Pour the batter evenly into each of the pans until it fills ¾ of the way up the shell. Place half a pear, round side up, into the middle of the batter. Place a piece of butter on top of each tart and place the baking sheet on the center rack of the oven. Bake for 15 minutes and remove. Gently remove the outer ring of the tart shells and run a knife around the bottom to remove.

Brandied caramel: In a heavy-bottomed saucepan over high heat, add the sugar, water and lemon juice. Whisk to incorporate the sugar. Continue to cook until the sugar mixture turns golden brown. Add the brandy and cook off the alcohol, about 10 seconds. Reduce the heat to low, stir in the cream, and cool in an ice bath.

To Serve: Place a warm tart in the center of 6 dessert plates. Spoon some of the brandied caramel around the plate. Place a scoop of ice cream on top of each tart and serve.

Lemon Souffle with Fresh Blueberry Coulis

Ingredients

Coulis

2 pints fresh blueberries

4 tablespoons granulated sugar

1 tablespoon fresh lemon juice

Fresh mint sprigs (for garnish)

Pudding

¾ cup + 6 teaspoons granulated sugar

5 tablespoons all-purpose flour

½ teaspoon kosher salt

3 eggs, separated

3¾ tablespoons fresh lemon juice, strained

2 lemons, zested

1 cup buttermilk

2 tablespoons unsalted butter, room temperature

Method

Coulis: In a sauce pot over medium heat, combine the blueberries, sugar and lemon juice. Cook until the blueberries are broken down halfway and their juice is slightly thick, about 20 minutes. Cool and reserve.

Pudding: Preheat the oven to 300°F. Lightly butter the inside of six 5-ounce ramekins. Sprinkle the inside of each ramekins with 1 teaspoon of sugar. Next, sift together the sugar, flour and salt. Using a standup mixer with whisk attachment, beat the egg whites to stiff peaks. Working quickly, transfer the whites to another container and set aside. With the paddle attachment, beat the egg yolks, lemon juice, lemon zest and buttermilk until incorporated. With the machine running, gradually add the sifted sugar, flour and salt until just incorporated. With a rubber spatula, fold in the egg whites until just incorpo- rated. (Note: Do not overmix or the egg whites will break down.) Fill each of the ramekins to the top with the pudding filling and transfer the ramekins to a deep baking dish. Fill the dish halfway up the sides of the ramekins with room temperature water. Wrap the entire dish with foil, but make sure to tent the foil, or the pudding will rise and stick to the foil. Place the dish on the center rack of the oven and cook for 45 minutes. Remove the foil and cook until the top turns golden brown, about 5 to 7 minutes.

To Serve: Run a paring knife along the inside edge of the ramekins and turn them over onto the middle of 6 dessert plates. Spoon some of the blueberry coulis around the dish and garnish with a mint sprig.

Note: You can make the pudding ahead of time and reheat for 5 minutes in a 400°F oven before serving. This dessert also goes well with whipped cream.

At Bis on Main, we like to hit 'singles,' not a home run every time.

Black Mission Fig Paste

MAKES 2½ CUPS

Ingredients

2 tablespoons olive oil

2 shallots, minced

2 cups dried black mission figs, stems off, quartered lengthwise

1½ cups ruby port wine

3 tablespoons balsamic vinegar

1 tablespoon granulated sugar

1 teaspoon kosher salt

½ teaspoon black pepper

Method

In a heavy-bottomed sauce pot over medium-high heat, add the olive oil. When hot, add the shallots. Saute until just brown, about 1 minute. Add the figs, tossing a couple times, and add the port wine, balsamic vinegar, sugar, salt and pepper. Reduce the heat to medium low and cook until the figs are soft and only ⅓ of the liquid remains, about 15 minutes. Transfer to a food processor and puree until smooth, yet thick. Cool and reserve. Serve chilled or at room temperature. (Note: This paste keeps very well when refrigerated.)

Note: This fig paste can be used as a wonderful compliment to a cheese platter in place of fresh fruit.

Apricot & Golden Raisin Marmalade

MAKES 3 CUPS

Ingredients

2 tablespoons olive oil

4 tablespoons fennel bulb, small diced

1 tablespoon minced shallot

1 cup golden raisins

1 cup dried apricots, medium diced

2 tablespoons granulated sugar

⅛ cup white wine vinegar

2 cups sweet wine (riesling or muscat)

1 teaspoon kosher salt

¼ teaspoon black pepper

2 tablespoons fresh lemon juice

Method

In a saucepan over medium-high heat, add the olive oil. When hot, add the fennel and shallots, and sweat, stirring frequently, until translucent, about 3 minutes. Add the raisins, apricots, sugar and vinegar. Stir and cook for 1 minute. Add the wine, salt, pepper and lemon juice. Cook until the fruit is plump and appears glossy, about 10 to 12 minutes. Transfer half of the mixture to a food processor, and puree until a paste is achieved. Fold the puree back in with the other fruit, and cool. Serve chilled or at room temperature.

Black Currant & Cranberry Jam

MAKES 3 CUPS

Ingredients

2 tablespoons unsalted butter

4 tablespoons red onion, small diced

1 cup dried cranberries

1 cup dried black currants

3½ cups red wine

¼ cup red wine vinegar

1 teaspoon kosher salt

2 tablespoons granulated sugar

Sachet

Note: A sachet is a fabric bag filled with herbs and spices and tied off with a piece of kitchen string.

2 strips of orange peel

2 juniper berries

1 star anise

6 black peppercorns

Method

In a saucepan over medium-high heat, add the butter. When the butter is melted, add the diced red onion and sauté till translucent, about 3 minutes. Add the cranberries and currants, and stir for 30 seconds. Add the red wine, red wine vinegar, salt, sugar and the sachet. Stir several times. Bring to a simmer, then reduce heat to medium and continue to cook until liquid reduces down to the level of the solid ingredients, about 15 to 20 minutes. Remove and discard the sachet. Transfer half of the mixture to a food processor, and run until the mixture forms a thick paste. Transfer the mixture back into the pan with the solids, stir to incorporate, and cool. Store in an airtight container refrigerated for up to 3 weeks.

Rhubarb & Bing Cherry Chutney

MAKES ABOUT 3 CUPS

Ingredients

1 tablespoon olive oil

3 rhubarb stalks, small diced

½ red onion, peeled and small diced

1 teaspoon fresh ginger, finely diced

½ cup red wine vinegar

2 cups dried sour cherries (pulsed 5 times in a food processor)

3 cups red wine

1½ teaspoon kosher salt

½ teaspoon black pepper

¼ cup granulated sugar

¼ cup Dr Pepper

Method

In a sauce pot, over medium-high heat, add the oil. When the oil is hot, add the rhubarb, onion and ginger; sauté until lightly caramelized, about 8 minutes. Add the red wine vinegar and reduce by half. Add the cherries, red wine, salt, pepper and sugar. Reduce the heat to medium and simmer until the cherries are plump and the mixture has softened, about 15 minutes. Add the Dr Pepper and cook 5 additional minutes. Remove from heat and cool. Keep refrigerated.

Note: Yes, the recipe does call for Dr Pepper. Strangely enough, the flavor of the soda blends well with the cherry and ginger and aids in creating the right viscosity for the chutney.

Candied Nuts

Ingredients

2 quarts canola frying oil

½ cup powdered sugar

¼ teaspoon cayenne pepper

1 teaspoon kosher salt

2 cups of walnut halves, hazelnuts, pecan halves, or any nut of choice

Method

Bring a large sauce pot of water to a boil.

In a heavy-bottomed, high-sided pot for frying, add the canola oil over medium-high heat until a temperature of 350°F is achieved (use a candy thermometer). Make sure the oil only comes halfway up the side of the pot. When the oil reaches temperature, reduce the heat to medium-low.

In a mixing bowl, combine the sugar, cayenne and salt. Mix to incorporate. When the water comes to a boil, gently add the nuts and blanch for 30 seconds. Remove the nuts from the water and drain on paper towel. While the nuts are still hot, toss them in the dry mixture, coating them thoroughly. Shake off the excess mixture and transfer the coated nuts to the frying oil. The oil will rise and bubble violently for a moment. Fry the nuts for 90 seconds, remove from the oil and transfer to a cooling rack. Do not refrigerate the nuts. The candied nuts will keep well in a covered container for 3 weeks.

index